LUDWIG WITTGENSTEIN

Ludwig Wittgenstein

Philosophy in the Age of Airplanes

ANTHONY GOTTLIEB

Yale
UNIVERSITY
PRESS
New Haven and London

Yale University Press books may be purchased in quantity for educational, business, or promotional use. For information, please e-mail sales.press@yale.edu (U.S. office) or sales@yaleup.co.uk (U.K. office).

Set in Janson Oldstyle type by Integrated Publishing Solutions.
Printed in the United States of America.

Library of Congress Control Number: 2025931248
ISBN 978-0-300-18047-3 (hardcover)

A catalogue record for this book is available from the British Library.

Authorized Representative in the EU: Easy Access System Europe, Mustamäe tee 50, 10621 Tallinn, Estonia, gpsr.requests@easproject.com

10 9 8 7 6 5 4 3 2 1

Frontispiece: Ludwig Wittgenstein, circa 1908.
(Pictorial Press Ltd / Alamy Stock Photo)

ALSO BY ANTHONY GOTTLIEB

The Dream of Reason: A History of Western Philosophy from the Greeks to the Renaissance

The Dream of Enlightenment: The Rise of Modern Philosophy

In memory of my father, Felix Gottlieb
(Vienna, 1922–London, 2016)

It is impossible for me to say in my book one
word about all that music has meant in my life.
How then can I hope to be understood?
—Ludwig Wittgenstein to Maurice Drury

CONTENTS

LUDWIG WITTGENSTEIN

1

"A New Way of Philosophizing"

In 1931, at the age of forty-one, Ludwig Wittgenstein mused in his diary that perhaps his name would live on only as the end point of Western philosophy—"like the name of the one who burnt down the library of Alexandria."[1] There probably was no such an arsonist. The books of ancient Alexandria seem to have perished mainly by rot and neglect, not in a single blaze. And Western philosophy certainly did not come to an end with Wittgenstein, who died in 1951. He did not really believe that it would. Wittgenstein could get carried away when writing in his diaries, especially when contemplating himself, which he did often.

But he did think that he had found a fresh approach to philosophical problems. At least for a while and in some places, his influence changed how philosophy was done. A memorial brass in Trinity College, Cambridge, that stands on a wall behind statues of Isaac Newton and Francis Bacon declares (in Latin):

"Ludwig Wittgenstein, Fellow of this College, Professor of Philosophy in the University for eight years, showed to many a new way of philosophizing . . . and taught by examples that reason should be freed from the snares of language."[2]

In his book *Tractatus Logico-Philosophicus*, which he wrote while on military service in the 1914–18 war, Wittgenstein proclaimed that the problems of philosophy arise only because "the logic of our language is misunderstood." Once this logic had been laid bare, the problems would be resolved once and for all, or so he then believed. He later came to think of philosophy as a never-ending form of therapy: it will be a continuing "battle against the bewitchment of our intelligence by means of language."[3]

Wittgenstein once wrote that the business of philosophy is to "soothe the mind about meaningless questions." He was echoing a passage from *The Principles of Mechanics*, published in 1894 by a physicist, Heinrich Hertz, which suggested that some questions about force and electricity are based on confusion and should be addressed not directly but by exposing the muddles that lay behind them. Such queries, Hertz wrote, "will not have been answered; but our minds, no longer vexed, will cease to ask illegitimate questions." Wittgenstein's fundamental idea was to apply this thought to philosophy. He read Hertz when he was a teenager and liked quoting him to family and friends, mentioning this passage often in writings and talks. He once said that it seemed to him to "sum up philosophy."[4]

Philosophical questions had not usually been regarded as illegitimate or meaningless—not, at least, by philosophers. So this was quite a departure from traditional conceptions of the subject. Perhaps it was time for one. As Wittgenstein once put it to a friend: "Why should philosophy in the age of airplanes and automobiles be the same . . . as in the age when people travelled by coach or on foot?"[5]

* * *

When he first arrived in Cambridge, on 18 October 1911, Wittgenstein was a twenty-two-year-old Austrian-born student of aeronautical engineering at the University of Manchester. He had made an appointment to visit the philosopher Bertrand Russell at Trinity College because he was interested in Russell's writings about logic and the philosophy of mathematics. He never returned to engineering after this meeting. Eight months later, Russell astonished Wittgenstein's eldest sister, Hermine, by telling her, "We expect the next big step in philosophy to be taken by your brother."[6]

In the decades after his death, Ludwig Wittgenstein came to be seen as one of the leading thinkers of the century. But in his lifetime, he was not the famous member of his family. Outside the small world of philosophy, the better-known Wittgensteins were, first, Ludwig's father, Karl, a Viennese industrialist who died in 1913, and then one of Ludwig's brothers, Paul, a concert pianist whose international career began in the 1920s.

In 1913, *The Economist* called Karl Wittgenstein "the most prominent person in the history of modern Austrian industry." The "Carnegie of Austria," as he was widely known, wrote provocative newspaper columns and delivered speeches to businessmen in America. At home, his fame made him a target of the Viennese satirist and critic Karl Kraus, whose journal, *Die Fackel*, portrayed him as a thieving speculator and exploiter of the working man, and twice compared him to Phineas Barnum, a notorious American showman.[7] But most of Karl Wittgenstein's press was more positive. On the day after his death, Vienna's leading daily, *Die Neue Freie Presse*, devoted almost as much space to his patronage of the arts as it did to his business career. Karl was the principal backer of the Viennese "Secession" movement—a group of young artists, including Gustav Klimt, who saw themselves as seceding from the artistic establishment. The family's townhouse, known to outsiders as the Palais Wittgenstein, was one of Vienna's leading music salons. The city's most celebrated living composer, Brahms, who was friendly with several members of two generations of the Wittgenstein family, lived around the corner from the Palais and visited often.

There were many amateur musicians in the family, but the only one to make a career of music was Karl's second-youngest child, Paul. For more than three decades, Paul played the halls of Vienna, Berlin, Paris, London, New York, and many other places from Athens to Zagreb. He performed under the batons of the grandest conductors, including Richard Strauss and Bruno Walter, both of whom were family friends, and of rising stars, such as the young Leonard Bernstein and Sir Adrian Boult. Some of the attention Paul received from the world's press was due to a sensational oddity: he played with only one hand. His right arm had been amputated at the elbow while he was serving in the Austrian army in 1914. With heroic determination, Paul developed techniques that enabled him to become a concert pianist despite his injury. "After the first few moments of wondering how the devil he had accomplished it," wrote the *New York Herald Tribune* in a concert review, "one almost forgot that one was listening to a player whose right sleeve hung empty at his side."[8] Paul used his family's wealth to commission one-handed piano works from Ravel, Prokofiev, Richard Strauss, Benjamin Britten, and at least fourteen other composers.

When Ludwig Wittgenstein, Karl's youngest child, died in England in 1951, his obituary in the *Times* put him in the wrong family. The newspaper did not seem to realize that he was related to the Karl Wittgenstein or the Paul Wittgenstein who had featured in its pages, and it reported, incorrectly, that "his ancestors included the Prince Wittgenstein who fought against Napoleon."[9] Ludwig's distant paternal ancestors were in fact German Jewish merchants, not warlike princes. They came from a county in North Rhine–Westphalia that was named after the Sayn-Wittgenstein family, one member of which, Prince Peter of Sayn-Wittgenstein-Ludwigsburg-Berleburg, did indeed fight against Napoleon. The Jewish Wittgensteins adopted the name in the early nineteenth century. Later, Ludwig's paternal grandparents converted to Christianity. But like many converted former Jews and assimilated Jews in Europe at the time, their real religion was German culture, especially German music.

The *Times* likened Ludwig to "a religious contemplative of the hermit type." This was almost apt. He often sought solitude, retreating many times to an isolated house in Norway, and in later years to lonely spots in Ireland. In 1919, he gave away all of his money to some of his siblings, and thereafter lived a simple life, but in a complicated way. It was harder to cast off the restlessness that he shared with his father than it was to relinquish the wealth that he had inherited from him. After more or less abandoning philosophy at the end of the First World War, Ludwig trained to be an elementary-school teacher, spent time as a gardener's assistant in a monastery, and then taught in small towns in rural Austria. He gave up schoolmastering in April 1926, had another stint of gardening, then worked for two years as a self-taught architect, designing a house in Vienna for his youngest sister, Gretl. In 1929 he returned to Cambridge and philosophy, and mostly taught there until 1947, when he resigned his professorship. He spent his last years in guesthouses, hotels, borrowed cottages, or with friends. When he had been teaching in Cambridge, living in a spartan style, he was often tempted to leave and do something else. Among the alternatives he considered were manual labor on a collective farm in Russia, medicine, and psychiatry. In earlier life, he told Bertrand Russell, he had considered becoming a monk.

He would have been as unusual a monk as he was a philosopher. "I am not a religious man," Ludwig told a close friend, "but I can't help seeing everything from a religious point of view." When he was a soldier, he wrote in his notebooks that "Christianity is the only *sure* way to happiness," but he had little interest in Jesus and none in going to church. He had fallen under the influence of Tolstoy's watered-down *The Gospel in Brief*, in which Christianity is presented not as a divine revelation or even as a historical phenomenon but as "a teaching that gives meaning to life." Wittgenstein often read the New Testament. He still buzzed around it like an "insect around the light," as he put it nearly twenty-five years after first encountering Tolstoy's *Gospel.* And there were many occasions when he prayed fervently. But it is not clear to whom or what he was praying. Hermine reported in 1918 that "Ludwig knows no external God." A Catholic friend's opinion was that he "did not adhere to any form of Christian belief."[10]

To Ludwig, the notion of God was above all "the thought of the fearful judge." Tormented by his own shortcomings, he yearned for a salvation that he often expressed in terms of a desire to be *anständig*—decent or upstanding. He sometimes used the language of religion to articulate his guilt and his hopes, which is perhaps one reason why he said that he saw things from a religious point of view: "I am a worm, but through God I will become a man," as he put it in a wartime notebook.[11]

He berated himself above all for vanity and conceit. He was, as he acknowledged, vain even about his own vices, noting in his diary that hardly any of his self-reproaches were "written *entirely* without the feeling that at least it is nice that I see my faults." Sometimes he was too hard on himself, apologizing abjectly for trivial matters and regretting flaws that probably only he saw. In 1931 he wrote in a notebook that "I am uncommonly cowardly, & I behave in life like a coward in battle."[12] Yet he did not behave like a coward in battle when he actually was in battle. He was decorated for bravery several times during his military service.

It was, if not vanity, then at least a remarkable degree of self-belief that enabled the twenty-two-year-old Ludwig to seek out Bertrand Russell and debate with him as an equal. This was at a time when Wittgenstein knew little philosophy and had no qualifications except an engineering diploma from Berlin and an undistinguished school record. A similar self-assured determination marked his later career. He scorned the idea that academic regulations should apply to him, and he set out to refashion philosophy according to his own lights. The one-armed pianism of his brother Paul showed what the iron will of a Wittgenstein could achieve when he set out to do things in his own way. Their father set an example for both of them. Karl's obituary in the *Neue Freie Presse* noted that his way of life was "thoroughly original and conducted in a style that he himself had created" and that he had "an inborn lack of respect for authorities and conventions."[13] But not every Wittgenstein managed to make his own way. Paul and Ludwig were the only two of Karl's five sons who did not kill themselves.

2

At Home with the Wittgensteins

Ludwig Wittgenstein told a story about sitting in the family home in Vienna while his brother Paul was playing the piano in another room. Suddenly the music stopped. Paul burst in on Ludwig and exclaimed: "I can't play when you are in the house. I feel your scepticism seeping under the door."[1]

It is a plausible tale. According to the servants at the Palais Wittgenstein, there were often rows when the two brothers were at home. The arguments may not all have been about music, but many of them will have been. Paul's playing was often criticized by his siblings and by their mother—"Must he pound the piano like that?" she once asked. And Ludwig was habitually outspoken in his musical verdicts. "They play like pigs" was his comment on hearing that a distinguished string quartet was coming to Cambridge. A friend who had often seen Ludwig give advice on musical and other matters claimed that "whenever he was not *completely* sure of his ground, he would not open his mouth." But Ludwig seems frequently to have been sure of his ground, and he could radiate reproach. Fania Pascal, who taught him Russian in Cambridge in the 1930s, began a memoir of Wittgenstein by noting that it was impossible to write about him "without being almost physically aware of his disapproval and scathing glance."[2]

Music was not just a pastime in the house where Ludwig and his seven siblings were raised. It served as currency in their dealings with one another. Of the several hundred letters, postcards, and telegrams that the family exchanged in the first half of the twentieth century—a period encompassing two wars, civil unrest in Vienna, Nazi harassment, and family dramas—over a third find room to mention musical works or performances. "I went to hear Bach's *Mass in B minor* yesterday, I almost fell to my knees." "You were also in my thoughts during the final rehearsal of the Labor quintet." "Mama . . . is playing a beautiful Schubert quartet for four hands with Kurt at the moment."[3]

Mama—Leopoldine or "Poldy" Wittgenstein—communicated with her children through music, the only language in which she was fluent. Ludwig said that she had never brought a thought to completion except at the piano. She could sight-read and transpose any difficult piece of music, explained her eldest daughter, Hermine, in a family memoir, but "it would have been impossible for her to grasp swiftly a complicated sentence made up of words." As a child, Poldy used to delight her father by returning from the opera and playing from memory what she had just heard, sometimes falling off the piano stool in excitement. As a mother, Poldy had, in Hermine's opinion, "no real understanding of the eight quirky children to whom she gave birth."[4] Her bond with them consisted of musical games and of playing to and with them at the keyboard. In her seventies, Poldy wrote to Ludwig that she was spending at least three hours each day playing piano duets with members of the family.

Perhaps the quirkiest of her offspring was her eldest son,

Hans, who had "nothing but music in his head" from earliest childhood, according to Hermine.[5] Hans was a budding composer at the age of four and played the violin each Sunday in St. Peter's Church at the age of nine. The family proudly collected anecdotes of his precocity and eccentricity—he was said to have been pronounced a genius by Julius Epstein, a professor at the Vienna Conservatory who had taught Mahler. Hans vanished from a boat somewhere in the United States in his mid-twenties, presumed to have killed himself. He did not want the career in industry on which his father insisted.

For Ludwig, who was about twelve when Hans died, his eldest brother's all-consuming dedication to his art was a model of how one should live. He once recalled being woken at three in the morning by the sound of Hans, wild and engrossed, playing one of his compositions. Ludwig admiringly recounted to Bertrand Russell a similar tale that had been told of Beethoven's manic absorption. Beethoven and Mozart were "the actual sons of God," he wrote to Russell in 1912. After being subjected to one of Ludwig's own intense emotional fits, another Cambridge friend noted in his diary in 1913 that he was "as bad . . . as people like Beethoven were," which Ludwig would have taken as the best sort of compliment.[6] Beethoven was also venerated by Paul, whose principal teacher, Theodor Leschetizky, had studied under a pupil of Beethoven's. And Karl Wittgenstein was particularly proud of owning a controversial marble bust of a fierce, bare-chested Beethoven as well as a collection of Beethoven's manuscripts and letters.

Beethoven was long dead by the time Ludwig and Paul were born, but connections—some close, some distant, all pleasing—could be traced by the Wittgenstein family to him and to many of the other composers who were revered at the Palais. Beethoven's friend Franz Grillparzer, who wrote the oration for his burial and was one of his pallbearers, became a good friend of Ludwig's paternal grandfather, Hermann Wittgenstein, and was a frequent guest at the salons of Hermann's wife, Fanny, née Figdor. In 1844, Mendelssohn, whose *Songs without Words* were later played "over and over again" at the Palais, according to a family friend, wrote to thank Hermann and Fanny for introducing him to Joseph Joachim, a violin prodigy whose performance of Beethoven's violin concerto at the age of twelve under Mendelssohn's baton had been a sensation.[7]

Joachim was a first cousin of Ludwig's grandmother Fanny, who had taken him to live with her so that she could further his musical career. Joachim brought his friends Brahms and Robert and Clara Schumann into the Wittgenstein family circle. Two of Ludwig's aunts took piano lessons from Brahms. There was also a link with Schubert, whose works became particular favorites of Ludwig's. Schubert's close friend Leopold Kupelwieser, a painter for whose marriage Schubert wrote a waltz, had two sons: one married one of Ludwig's aunts and the other gave Ludwig's father his start in the steel industry.

When Ludwig's parents held their own musical salons at the Palais from the early 1890s, Brahms and Clara were regular guests. Robert Schumann had died in 1856, but he was there in spirit: his lush secular oratorio *Paradise and the Peri* was Poldy's favorite piece of music. There were still Schumanns in the house many years later. In the 1930s, a piano pupil of Paul's was dumbfounded to learn that an elderly lady who had overheard one of her lessons in the Palais was Schumann's youngest daughter. Brahms's visits to the Palais in his last years were remembered by some of Ludwig's siblings as a great honor, though his youngest sister, Gretl, shuddered in adulthood at the memory of Brahms jovially sprinkling champagne on her hair when she was nine, to the great amusement of her parents and their guests.

Ludwig once declared that music "came to a full stop with Brahms." He was echoing the sentiments of his mother's friend Eduard Hanslick, Vienna's leading music critic, who had confessed in his autobiography that, as far as he was concerned,

Music room of the Palais Wittgenstein.
(© Françoise and Pierre Stonborough / Wittgenstein Initiative)

music "culminates in Beethoven, Schumann and Brahms." For Ludwig and Paul, the greatest music was the music of their childhood home. Both were skeptical of much of what came afterward. "You are a musician of the nineteenth century, I am of the twentieth," Prokofiev wrote to Paul, who had commissioned a concerto from the Russian composer but could not understand it and never performed it.[8]

One musician whose works Ludwig and Paul always championed was Josef Labor, a blind organist and pianist who had been court musician to the last king of Hanover and later became house composer to the Palais Wittgenstein. Nearly all of Labor's works after 1915 were written for Paul, and the whole family was infatuated with him. When Ludwig was dying in Cambridge in 1951, several of his last letters concerned the fate of a drawing that his sister Hermine had made of Labor in 1924.

Ludwig was anxious that the original should end up in the right hands, and he wanted a good copy to be sent to him. Paul, too, though living in New York from 1938 until his death in 1961, never left behind the sounds of their home in Vienna. An American friend of Paul's recalled that "although the palace was gone and Brahms was dead, he was in that world. . . . That was his milieu."[9]

A painting by Klimt of a knight in gold armor standing erect in the stirrups of his horse was displayed in the Palais Wittgenstein when Ludwig was a teenager, sometimes at the top of the marble staircase climbed by guests on their way to Karl and Poldy's salons. Karl bought the picture, called *The Golden Knight*, also known as *Life Is a Struggle*, in 1903. He was a keen equestrian himself. In her memoir, Hermine described Karl as "a strong, well-built man, a good swordsman, a good horseman. He was a man whose energy and boldness could be seen at a hundred paces."[10]

One of Karl's bold acts was to import aggressive business methods to a relatively backward Austria, which made this golden knight an "Amerikaner" to some, as Vienna's *Neue Freie Presse* noted. The newspaper also dubbed him "ein Selfmademan."[11] The term does not mean quite the same in German as it does in English. Karl Wittgenstein made his own rules and made his own way, but his tale was not one of rags to riches. It was one of riches to many more riches.

Karl's father was born Herz (or Hirsch) Moses Meier, the son of a land agent in the Jewish community of Korbach in northern Germany in 1802. In about 1808, the family name became Wittgenstein; at some stage, Herz became Hermann, and he added the middle name "Christian" after his Protestant baptism in 1839. Looking back as a wealthy Christian proprietor and landowner, he wrote in his will, "I began my career in other and troublesome circumstances."[12]

Hermann began as a wool merchant and made an advantageous marriage. His wife, Fanny Figdor, came from a distinguished family of Jewish merchants and bankers who had lived in Vienna since the late eighteenth century, a time when few Jews were permitted to do so. By the early twentieth century, the Figdors owned one of the most significant private art collections in Europe. After his marriage, Hermann went into business with the Figdors: their joint ventures included property, construction, building materials, timber, brown coal, and agricultural products. And he held salons, as his parents-in-law had done; most of the Wittgensteins' grandest musical connections came via the Figdors.

Hermann Wittgenstein also managed and developed noblemen's estates, acquiring a taste for living on such estates himself. Hermann and Fanny's children were brought up in castles and behaved accordingly. Brahms found them rather grand. At home, Brahms remarked, the Wittgensteins "go about as if at court."[13]

Hermine attributed her father's own fondness for "oversized rooms" to his childhood in castles. The noble manner that Brahms observed in Hermann's household was evident in his descendants, too. An "imperious" demeanor was one student's first impression of Ludwig in Cambridge in the mid-1930s. His "whole personality was commanding," wrote another. A piano student of Paul's was startled when Paul once swept his hands away from the keyboard in annoyance, but the pupil came to see it as "just his patrician way." In 1920, Hermine and Paul found it ridiculous of Ludwig to think that he could pass for an ordinary person in the village where he was then a schoolmaster. Paul scolded him in a letter: "Given the unbelievable degree to which our name is known . . . the properties we own spread across the whole of Austria, the various charitable causes we're involved in, etc., etc., it is impossible, truly perfectly impossible, that any person bearing our name, and whose distinguished and refined up-bringing anyone can see from a thousand feet off, will not be recognised as a member of our family." When Gretl visited Chicago in the same year, a newspaper described her as a countess, presumably because she acted like one.[14]

Hermine never met their paternal grandfather, Hermann, but recorded that he had "a certain rigidness and formality . . . which were not mitigated by warmth." By all accounts, Hermann was industrious, righteous, and strict, which has led some writers about the Wittgenstein family to describe him, and Karl, as embodying the values of German Protestantism.[15] This may reflect how they saw themselves, but there is no reason to regard the virtues exemplified by Hermann or Karl as more typical of German Protestants than of German Jews.

Hermine was under the impression that her paternal grandparents had been baptized before their marriage, but this seems to have been a family myth. Hermann and Fanny were married as Jews in Vienna on 27 November 1839, according to records held by Vienna's Jewish community.[16] This was a few weeks before their baptisms in Germany, where they went to live from the end of 1839 to 1851. It is not known why the couple bothered with a Jewish marriage when they were about to convert and live as Christians. Perhaps it was to please Fanny's parents, Wilhelm and Amalia Figdor, who were active in Jewish religious and philanthropic life and were buried in a Jewish cemetery.

Accounts of the Wittgenstein family commonly describe Hermann as antisemitic, though the sole evidence for this is a tainted source from the Nazi era. It is a letter written in September 1938 to a Nazi ministry by one of his descendants who sought a favorable racial classification for the family by claiming that Hermann was the illegitimate offspring of a prince. Similar petitions were not uncommon: Jewish mothers sometimes tried to save their children by pretending to have had adulterous liaisons with non-Jews. In support of the idea that Hermann cannot really have been Jewish, the author of this letter, a granddaughter of one of Ludwig's aunts, offered several arguments. One was that Hermann and his offspring did not look Jewish. Photographs were enclosed. Such considerations did sometimes sway the authorities, who regarded a Jewish appearance as a scientifically determinable matter. Another argument was that Hermann was, she wrote, "known as an antisemite, who strictly avoided dealings with Vienna's Jewish circles, and did not permit his children to marry Jews." She correctly noted that of Hermann's nine married children, only one (Karl) married a "half-breed"; the rest all married "pure Aryans."[17]

Since Hermann was in partnership with the Figdors when he lived in Vienna from the late 1850s, he can hardly be said to have shunned Vienna's Jews. He may or may not have been an antisemite himself, but he would have known that the world in which his descendants would have to make their way was an antisemitic one. This was perhaps reason enough to hope that they would not marry Jews. In 1851, when Hermann, Fanny, and their first eight children moved to Austria, living at first outside Vienna, the emperor reinstated many anti-Jewish discriminatory laws that had been dropped a few years earlier. Legal restrictions on Austrian Jews were lifted in the 1860s, but it was easier to change laws than attitudes. Vienna grew steadily more antisemitic following Hermann's death in 1878, especially after an influx in the 1880s of Jews fleeing pogroms in the east. These eastern Jews often stood out because of their distinctive clothing and language. Although Jews had been established in Berlin, Hamburg, and other German cities for several hundred years, Vienna's Jewish population arrived suddenly. By 1889, the year of Ludwig's birth, it had grown in just four decades from almost nothing to 12 percent of the city's population. Militantly antisemitic parties began to dominate Vienna's politics in the 1890s when Hermann's grandchildren were growing up. "Thank God, the majority of this House is antisemitic!" shouted Eduard von Stransky, a member of Austria's parliament, during a debate in 1908 about Jewish quotas in schools and universities.[18]

In 1921, some forty thousand people attended an international congress of antisemitic organizations in Vienna. The next year, *City without Jews: A Novel from the Day After Tomorrow* was published. In this partly prophetic satire by Hugo Bettauer, a Jewish-born writer, Austria expels all of its Jews, whereupon Vienna dwindles into an impoverished backwater and the Jews are invited to return. In the real Austria, Bettauer was murdered by a Nazi in 1925, the country began systematically to persecute its Jews after being annexed by Germany in 1938, and Bettauer's eldest son died in Auschwitz.

By the time of Ludwig's generation, the Wittgensteins understandably regarded themselves as no longer Jewish, sometimes snobbishly distancing themselves from Jews: "The wife is especially nice, although of course Jewish," wrote Hermine to Ludwig in 1939 about a family they had helped. If the siblings were ever aware that their father had been labeled "the Jew Wittgenstein" by the antisemitic press, they succeeded in ignoring it. Karl was given a large hooked nose in a cartoon in 1897, the same year in which the recently baptized Mahler was derided for his "Jew-boy antics on the podium."[19]

According to Nazi racial laws, people with at least three Jewish grandparents were "full Jews" themselves, regardless of their religion. Even Catholic priests and nuns were sometimes ruled to be Jews. Because Poldy's Jewish-born father had, like Hermann and Fanny, converted only in adulthood, Ludwig and his siblings counted as fully Jewish in Nazi terms, the only grandchildren of Hermann and Fanny to do so.

"From his earliest youth, my son Karl has gone his own way, unlike his siblings, though in the end this has not been particularly to his disadvantage."[20] Thus began Hermann's first letter to Karl's fiancée, Poldy, whom he had not yet met. He welcomed her to the family, but only after this somewhat grumpy remark. The young Karl had certainly been a handful and a cause for concern. The youngest son of eleven children, he was the family jester and chief mischief-maker in a strict home, where failure to practice the piano could result in confinement to the music room, and worse offenses sentenced one to imprisonment in darkness. The young Karl used an unseaworthy laundry tub to circumnavigate the moat of Schloss Vösendorf, the castle south of Vienna where the family lived in his early youth, and he once interfered with the castle's clock tower to make it strike all night.

Karl ran away from one school at the age of eleven and was expelled from another school six years later, apparently for denying the immortality of the soul. His parents decided to complete his education at home with tutors, but Karl had other plans. In January 1865, at the age of seventeen, he absconded with just his violin and some money obtained from his eldest sister. The family did not hear from him for about nine months. For the first two months of his adventure, he lived secretly in lodgings in Vienna, and then made his way to America, arriving penniless in New York on a ship from Hamburg in April 1865.

A fellow passenger got him his first job, as a waiter in a restaurant on Broadway. Soon he was playing his violin in restaurants, accompanied on the piano by an Austrian schoolteacher, and joined a "minstrel-troupe," as he described it.[21] Then he worked as a helmsman on a canal boat shipping pressed straw to Washington, DC, where he worked as a barman. Back in New York, his former accompanist recommended him for a position teaching violin and mathematics at a Catholic college, which was followed by jobs at other schools in New York teaching Greek, Latin, and technical drawing as well as music and mathematics.

In letters to his siblings, Karl confessed that he was too ashamed to write to his parents and would not be ready to ask for their forgiveness until he had some progress to report. "I have only one wish . . . to be on better terms with Papa," he wrote to his brother Louis in October 1865. Three months later, he had some good news to report—"This is the best time I've had in America. I'm decently dressed and always in decent company"—though he was not quite ready to return. He wrote to his mother that he felt shame and remorse, begging her to "speak to Papa on my behalf."[22]

When Karl arrived home at the beginning of 1867, the nineteen-year-old seemed to his siblings to be unwell, much changed, and conflating English and German in his speech. He was sent to recuperate at one of the farms rented by his father in what is now Romania, returning in the autumn to Vienna, where he began to study engineering. This seems to have been his mother's idea. He attended Vienna's polytechnic institute in the mornings, skipping subjects that he regarded as unnecessary, and spent the afternoons in a factory working as a technical draughtsman for the state railways. He left the institute without qualifications in 1868, but he was already a reformed character. For the next four years, Karl diligently gathered experience in engineering and draughtsmanship in several parts of the Austro-Hungarian Empire. In late 1872, when he was twenty-five, his rise began in earnest when he was given a job in the steel industry by Paul Kupelwieser, the brother-in-law of one of his sisters.

Kupelwieser had not expected much of this "restless young man," but he found Karl to be "an extraordinarily able and industrious" worker.[23] Employed at first to draw up plans for a steel mill in Teplitz (now in the Czech Republic), Karl was soon entrusted with managerial and commercial tasks at the new mill. By the time he was thirty, he was its managing director and part owner, having used money from his mother and from Poldy, whom he had married in 1874, to accumulate its stock. While he was in charge, Karl mounted a series of business coups that lay somewhere on the border between audacity and sharp practice.

In the late 1870s, he beat off competitors, including the giant firm of Krupp, to supply a planned Russian railroad in the Balkan Peninsula by convincing the Russians not to buy the type of rails they had had in mind but to use instead a lighter gauge that his mill had in stock for another customer. A couple of years later, in his mid-thirties, Karl exploited the overconfidence of a rival bidder to secure the exclusive Bohemian rights to a new English process for refining pig iron. The defeated rival thereby suffered such a setback that Karl was able to buy the firm—mostly with the company's own money—by outwitting one of its bookkeepers.

Other triumphs followed at a steady pace. By the time he was fifty, Karl ruled an integrated empire of mines, ironworks, steelworks, and hardware manufacturers, and sat on the boards of banks. He was an industrial baron of the stature of his American friends Andrew Carnegie and Charles M. Schwab, both of whom he entertained in Vienna.[24]

There was something "very un-Austrian" about Karl's "overly energetic manner," in the opinion of his daughter Hermine.[25] He had complained to her that in bureaucratic Austria, unlike America, entrepreneurs were seen merely as money-grubbers. Little credit was given for the intellectual skills and risk-taking required of his craft. The government, he began to feel, was nipping at his heels, and its hostility toward him was damaging the businesses he ran. So Karl cashed out and moved on. In 1898, he resigned from several directorships, and a year later, by the time he was fifty-two, had withdrawn from active business life. He moved his wealth into property and foreign stocks, and occupied himself with travel, hunting, riding, fencing, reading Latin classics, and his patronage of the arts. Karl also dispensed opinions on world affairs by writing articles and letters to newspapers and delivering speeches.

"A state that wants a large and healthy industry," he wrote five years after his retirement, "must accept the association of

Karl Wittgenstein in 1908.
(© Françoise and Pierre Stonborough / Wittgenstein Initiative)

capital on the most liberal and modern basis, and it must accept its dark sides as well." The defense of unfettered capitalism, though not of free trade, was a recurring motif in his writings. He was opposed to legislation that sought to protect consumers from cartels or fraud. Such laws, in his opinion, interfere with the work of entrepreneurs, who will ultimately lift the standard of living for everyone. These invaluable entrepreneurs need an appetite for danger and uncertainty: they must be ready to "stake everything on a single card," even at the risk of having to start again with nothing, as he explained in a lecture about the United States. Much is demanded of the workers as well as their bosses because constant improvement in the machinery they operate makes their jobs hard. Karl's interest in machines came to be shared by his youngest son, Ludwig, but although Ludwig was fascinated by mechanical things, he disdained what he took to be the effects of machinery and industry on culture. Karl, by contrast, maintained that "the precise and speedy working of machines" was a uniquely powerful driver of human progress.[26]

Karl's writings and speeches touched on English colonialism, which he admired—the English had "done more in the last two hundred years for the dissemination of culture . . . than all other peoples combined"—and on tariffs, taxation, cartels, and relations between Austria and Hungary, among other things. He speculated on the causes of America's success, published a whimsical "fairy tale" about currencies in the form of a dialogue between banknotes in the pocket of a waiter, and made comments in passing on the intellectual and bodily superiority of Austrian women to American ones. But although he was outspoken in print and at the podium, he seems to have been rather reticent at home. According to Hermine, "In general, my father spoke remarkably little. He enjoyed making his little jests, but he seldom talked in a connected way because many subjects seemed to him too serious—or, in most cases, too boring—to have a conventional conversation about. If, for once, he did say something serious, it was almost as though he was doing so against his will. . . . Usually, a witticism put an end to it. His friends were used to this peculiarity, but strangers did not know what to make of it."[27]

Karl was not the only member of the Wittgenstein family whose table talk could be baffling to outsiders. Twelve years after his death, one young woman who was staying with the family recorded, "One dined and talked at great speed and the conversation seemed to me—and indeed really was—barely comprehensible." She did not explain what made it hard to understand the Wittgensteins, but an aside by Hermine about the family's manner of speech may shed some light on the matter, and it is worth noting because at least seven of Ludwig's pupils and friends later remarked on this quirk. Hermine wrote that she and her siblings "very often used comparisons to communicate with one another," giving as an example how Ludwig preferred a vivid analogy to a straight answer. After he had mystified the family by becoming an elementary-school teacher in rural Austria, she told him that this use of his philosophically trained mind was "like someone wanting to use a precision instrument to open a crate." He responded, "You remind me of someone who is looking through a closed window and cannot make sense of the odd movements of a passer-by; he doesn't know what a storm is raging outside and that this person may be managing to stay on his feet only with great difficulty." In this case, it is easy to see what Ludwig meant: his teaching job soothed torments of which his sister was unaware. But later on, when he was lecturing in Cambridge, his hearers often found it hard to understand what he was driving at with his stream of allegories, similes, "picturesque examples," and "almost abnormal imagery."[28]

It was "like hearing a parable without being able to draw the moral," wrote one pupil. Another complained that he "continuously speaks in similes (which are only partly actual examples). . . . If something does not become clear, he does not try to give an explanation in simple words but instead looks for a new simile." Ludwig even came to regard the vivid comparisons of his family's conversations as an invaluable boon to philosophizing: "Usually we think of similes as second-best things, but in philosophy they are the best thing of all," he told a student.[29]

Because Karl Wittgenstein had so successfully made himself, he set out to make his children, too, especially the sons. Their own feelings and natures went unheeded, and their mother, Poldy, was not competent, and perhaps not inclined, to intervene on their behalf. Her remedy for everything seems to have been more music. As Hermine saw it, the dissonance between her brothers and their father was the cause of what she called "the great tragedy" of their home:

> It was tragic that our parents, despite their great moral seriousness and sense of duty, were unable to form a unit with their children; tragic that my father had sons who were as different from him as if they had been adopted from a foundling home! It must have been a bitter disappointment to him that none of them wanted to follow in his footsteps and continue his life's work. But one of the greatest dissimilarities, and the most tragic, was the lack of vitality and will to live in his sons when they were young, and this lack was reinforced by their abnormal education. Two sons, Hans and Rudi, left the world voluntarily in his lifetime, and two others, Paul and Ludwig, were so close to doing the same that it was perhaps only by chance that they stayed in this world and were able to cope with life. . . .
>
> [My father] did not live to see the death of his second-oldest son, my brother Kurt, who shot himself without any evident reason during the last days of the First World War. . . . [Kurt] also carried the germ of disgust for life within himself.[30]

All eight of Karl and Poldy's children were taught at home by a procession of tutors and servants until 1903, when the two youngest, Paul and Ludwig, were sent to schools—Paul to an academic high school in Vienna and Ludwig to a less demanding institution in the town of Linz, about one hundred miles west of Vienna, where he lived in lodgings. According to one report, some twenty-six people had been employed to teach the Wittgenstein children over the years, and no good word has been recorded about any of them. Hermine recalled an "inept and grumpy governess" who was with the family for over two decades, and "tutors from whom we learned nothing." The children's "abnormal education" was Karl's idea. He had developed an intense dislike of schools, according to Hermine, and maintained that "the only subjects which a person must learn with any application are Latin and mathematics . . . anything else, such as geography, history etc may be acquired through reading." It was not until the suicide of his eldest son, Hans, that Karl seems belatedly to have realized that the sort of self-directed education that had suited him might not work for his children. Hermine observed that her father was eager to pass on the lessons he had learned from his own odyssey, but he did not understand that "it is something different if someone, obeying his own personality, goes his own adventurous way or if the will of the father is the only driving force."[31]

In 1912, Ludwig told Bertrand Russell that his father had been "disappointed in all his other sons" and was "very anxious this one should do something respectable like engineering and not waste his time over such nonsense as philosophy." It was only after Karl's death in 1913 that Ludwig fully resolved not to return to his studies in engineering. And even when he did break free, he still endorsed some of his late father's values. "My father was a businessman and I am a businessman too; I want my philosophy to be businesslike, to get something done," Ludwig several times told one Cambridge friend.[32]

Despite Karl's own love of music—he took his violin on business trips and played duets with Poldy from their courtship to his last illness—he disapproved so strongly of Hans's obsession with music that Gretl had to stand guard while her eldest brother worked secretly at his compositions in a cellar. Karl also opposed Paul's wish to be a professional pianist, at least at first. Paul later claimed that his father eventually became "entirely reconciled" to the idea, though his concert debut did not take place until a year after Karl's death.[33] Hostility toward the precarious profession of music was not, of course, limited to industrialists. Johann Strauss I, the composer of the Radetzky March, tried to prevent his sons from following him into musical careers, but failed in all three cases.

In a memoir about Vienna at the turn of the twentieth century, the writer Stefan Zweig noted that "even the mightiest dynasties find that their sons are unwilling to take over the banks, the factories, the established and secure businesses of their fathers."[34] Zweig was discussing Jewish families, but the phenomenon was not confined to them. Filial disenchantment with the spirit of commerce was the theme of Thomas Mann's widely known novel *Buddenbrooks*, which was published in 1901 and read by Ludwig, and probably by other member of the Wittgenstein family. *Buddenbrooks* recounts the decline of a dynasty of Protestant German merchants, which it depicts as a conflict between the world of business and the world of the arts, particularly music. The terms used by Hermine to describe her brothers' supposed lack of vitality echoed the language of Mann's novel, and perhaps to some extent she saw their tragedy through his eyes.

The details of Hans's death, at the age of about twenty-six, are uncertain: he disappeared from a boat somewhere in the United States during 1902, but it is not known exactly where or when. Nobody in the family seems to have doubted that he took his own life, and when newspapers reported the public suicide of his brother Rudi, aged twenty-two, in 1904, they wrote that Rudi was the second of Karl's sons to kill himself. According to these reports, Rudi walked into a bar in Berlin, ordered milk for himself and a cognac for the pianist, and requested a rendition of "Forsaken Am I," a plaintive popular song in which an Austrian peasant mourns his dead sweetheart. To the accompaniment of this maudlin waltz, Rudi swallowed cyanide and expired shortly afterward. He wrote in a farewell letter to his parents that a friend of his had died and that he did not want to stay in the world without him. There were also plausible reports that he "despaired" of his sexual disposition. Dr. Magnus Hirschfeld, a German doctor who campaigned for the decriminalization of homosexuality, revealed that Rudi had come to see his colleagues, but "our influence on him did not go far enough to prevent the young man's suicide."[35]

Rudi had been in Berlin to study chemistry at his father's behest, but his interests lay elsewhere. He was regarded in the family as the one with the strongest feeling for literature. His brother Kurt, the third of Karl and Poldy's sons to die by his own hand, was the only one to follow their father into industry (reluctantly, if Hermine's account is correct). He shot himself in late 1918, at the age of forty, as he and the troops under his command retreated from Italian forces. Various stories about the circumstances of his death circulated among the family; nobody seemed sure what had really happened on the battlefield.[36]

Some accounts of Habsburg Vienna claim that it had more suicides than any other city in Europe. The evidence for such a ranking is sketchy, but the number of Austrian intellectuals, artists, and members of their families who killed themselves between 1860 and 1938 was aptly called "astonishing" by a study that discussed some two dozen of the suicides. In 1910, the Vienna Psychoanalytic Society organized a symposium, chaired by Sigmund Freud, to discuss the problem of suicide among the young. According to the first speaker, history showed that suicide can be "contagious," and he mentioned several purported epidemics of it.[37] One was a supposed increase in suicides in Athens at the end of the fifth century B.C. Another was in Germany at the end of the eighteenth century in the wake of Goethe's novel *The Sorrows of Young Werther.* It was believed that many young people chose to follow the example of Werther, whom Goethe hinted had himself got the idea of suicide from a book.

The suicidal young Wittgensteins had plenty of examples to follow. Before the deaths of Hans, Rudi, and Kurt, a first cousin of the brothers had killed himself at the age of eighteen in 1892. Among many other young members of notable families in Vienna to kill themselves in the 1890s were Gustav Mahler's brother at the age of twenty-one, and a son of the philosopher-physicist Ernst Mach at the age of twenty. Six months before Rudi Wittgenstein's somewhat theatrical suicide in 1904, there had occurred the much-discussed suicide of Otto Weininger, a depressive philosophical writer whose death was sometimes presented as an act of intellectual integrity. Ludwig, fourteen at the time, afterward told friends how disturbed he had been by Weininger's death.

Three months before Ludwig's birth, suicide had been given a macabre form of imperial imprimatur when Crown Prince Rudolf, the heir apparent to Emperor Franz Joseph, shot himself and a young lover, Mary Vetsera, at his hunting lodge in January 1889 at the age of thirty. Poldy's friend Hanslick described the impact of the event in his autobiography: "The desperate, inconsolable agitation that seized the whole population . . . is indescribable. I have lived through the saddest catastrophes in Vienna: revolutions, disastrous military campaigns, the loss of provinces, murderous devastation by fire and flood—but none of this can remotely be compared to that horrible [day]."[38] The prince's seventeen-year-old partner in his suicide pact probably did not know that he had tried to persuade other women to die with him. Rudolf, who kept a skull and a revolver on his desk, spent his last night in Vienna with one of them. A few days before that—if one is to believe what a lady-in-waiting claimed a valet had overheard—the emperor told his son, "You are not worthy of becoming my successor." In his farewell note to his wife, Rudolf wrote that he was going "calmly into death, which alone can save my good name." In another letter, he wrote: "I must die. That is the only way to leave this world at least like a gentleman."[39]

There was no particular scandal from which the prince needed to clear his name, though his political enemies exploited tattle about his affairs with women and sneered that he was a "friend of the Jews."[40] According to a code of honor that still swayed some minds, suicide could lift the stain of many kinds of failure, and Rudolf seems to have felt that he had failed his father and the empire.

A quarter century after Rudolf's gentlemanly exit, Ludwig still inhabited a world from which old ideas of honor had not quite departed. In a wartime notebook of 1915, he noted that a row with an officer cadet "may well come to a duel between us."[41] A few years earlier, he told a friend that for years he had been ashamed of never daring to kill himself. Finding a vocation seemed to silence Ludwig's suicidal thoughts for a while, though they returned sporadically until he was in his forties. In 1912, Bertrand Russell reassured him that he had a gift for philosophy, and this gave him a purpose in life.

3

The Teacher Who Taught Himself

After spending his first fourteen years at home, Ludwig was sent to a provincial secondary school, where his academic performance was merely middling, and then to a technical high school in Germany to study mechanical engineering. Next he went to England "with a view to making an experimental study of aerodynamics," according to the records of Manchester University, where he did not follow any formal course of study but did invent and patent an unusual type of propeller. He became interested in philosophical questions about mathematics which, after three and a half years in Manchester, drew him to Cambridge, where he was admitted as a philosophy undergraduate at the age of twenty-two; four months later, his status changed to that of a research student, nominally under the supervision of Bertrand Russell, who had already come to the conclusion that his supposed pupil would "do the work I should do, and do it better."[1] In late 1913, Ludwig left Cambridge without taking a degree to work at philosophy on his own.

Like his father, he had his own ideas about education. "As you know, I can't stand the method by which engineering is taught," Ludwig wrote to his sister Hermine from Manchester at the age of nineteen. When he was a schoolmaster in his thirties, he ignored the curriculum, according to a colleague, and "went on his own way, wanting to find new methods of teaching." And in his forties and fifties, as a teacher of philosophy, he discouraged pupils from wasting time on texts because this would only hinder their own philosophizing. In his last years, he joked about how little philosophy he had read—and that the little he had read was too much. It was best to follow one's own path. He was, anyway, bad at studying, as he acknowledged. It seems that Ludwig could absorb only what appealed to him and what he could make his own. A schoolmaster who met him in 1919 immediately spotted the marks of an autodidact, noting in his diary that "Wittgenstein has thoroughly appropriated what he has read with pleasure. Knows a lot by heart and is *self-taught*."[2]

Even his music-making was homemade and unconventional. Instead of learning an instrument when he was a child, Ludwig developed the ability to whistle complex pieces of music. He was what the Viennese called a *Kunstpfeifer*, an artistic whistler. Such people usually performed folk tunes and popular music, like Prince Rudolf's coachman Josef Bratfisch, who whistled ballads for the prince and his lover in the billiard room of the imperial hunting lodge on the night of their deaths.[3] But Ludwig's whistling repertoire was classical. Friends mentioned his versions of Brahms's Variations on a Theme by Haydn, songs by Schubert and Schumann, parts of Beethoven's Seventh Symphony and of Mozart's Requiem, and more. Often he would whistle a vocal or instrumental part while a friend played the piano.

* * *

Karl Wittgenstein was presumably pleased to have at least one son who showed a prodigious interest in mechanical things. At the age of ten, Ludwig had examined the workings of a sewing machine and used pieces of wood and wire to make a model that "could actually sew a few stitches," according to Hermine. A photograph of him at the age of eleven shows him working at a lathe. His curiosity about aeronautics seems to have begun as early as his schooldays: "What became of the flying machine?" asked one of his schoolmasters a few years after Ludwig left.[4]

When he had first arrived at the school, Ludwig pronounced his fellow pupils to be "muck."[5] He had probably had little exposure to children other than his relatives and those from similar families. For their part, the muck found this somewhat sensitive and stiffly formal schoolmate to be a creature from another world, as one of them later told Gretl. His interests and reading were very different from theirs. Another, considerably worse, pupil at the school was Adolf Hitler, who was asked to leave; he later claimed that he had purposely neglected his schoolwork in order to avoid being sent into the civil service. He and Ludwig overlapped at the school for one year, but were two classes apart and may not have met.

While he was at the school, Ludwig lost his religious faith, apparently after conversations with Gretl, his most intellectual sister. He also turned, at the age of sixteen, to the ideas of Arthur Schopenhauer (1788–1860), a German thinker with a private income who looked down on nearly all university philosophers and wrote more attractively than any of them. Schopenhauer rejected the Judeo-Christian creator-god, but found wisdom in Hindu scriptures and some Buddhist ideas. His system of "ultra-pessimism," as one commentator called it in 1853, vividly incorporated a multitude of topics. The index of an English edition of his main work contains the entries Drapery, Dreams, Drinks, Dross, Drudgery, Druids . . . Optics, Optimism, Oracle, Orang-utans . . . Vapour, Vases, Vatican, and Vaudeville. Several generations of educated German speakers, drawn to Schopenhauer's beautiful descriptions of the ugliness of life, regarded him as the only philosopher one needed to read.[6]

Schopenhauer had a special appeal for musical families like the Wittgensteins because he credited music with special powers and transcendent insights. Its effect is "so very much more powerful and penetrating than is that of the other arts, for these others speak only of the shadow, but music of the essence." A composer "reveals the innermost nature of the world," Schopenhauer continued, "and expresses the profoundest wisdom in a language that his reasoning faculty does not understand." When Gretl was in her late teens, she and her brother Rudi formed a group to talk about Schopenhauer and some other modern thinkers; two decades later she was still noting down thoughts about him. Ludwig told friends at Cambridge that when he was a teenager, the philosophy of Schopenhauer "struck him as fundamentally right, if only a few adjustments and clarifications were made." In particular, he had been "greatly impressed by Schopenhauer's theory of the 'world as idea.'"[7]

Schopenhauer's principal treatise opens with the words:

> "The world is my idea:"—this is a truth which holds good for everything that lives and knows, though man alone can bring it into reflective and abstract consciousness. . . . If he really does this, he has attained to philosophical wisdom. It then becomes clear and certain to him that what he knows is not a sun and an earth, but only an eye that sees a sun, a hand that feels an earth; that the world which surrounds him is there only as idea, i.e., only in relation to something else, the consciousness, which is himself. . . . No truth therefore is more certain . . . than this, that all that exists for knowledge, and therefore this whole world, is only object in relation to subject, perception of a perceiver, in a word, idea.

Schopenhauer agreed with Immanuel Kant (1724–1804), who maintained in his *Critique of Pure Reason* that the world we know is not the world as it is in itself. We experience reality as it appears through the lens of our limited mind's eye. Thus, for each of us, the world is only our idea of it. But while Kant argued that the world in itself is beyond our comprehension, Schopenhauer believed he had discovered what it is. It is, somehow, *Wille* (will)—a striving in nature and in ourselves. If we look within and observe our own volitions and desires, we can begin to lift the veil of ideas and expose the incessant endeavor that permeates all things. Nature's striving, including our own, is blind, unstoppable, and doomed. It is as if the universe were designed to produce failure and woe, for "misfortune in general is the rule." Our desires may sometimes be satisfied, but only fleetingly, "like the alms thrown to a beggar, which reprieves him today so that his misery may be prolonged till tomorrow." Moreover, getting what one wants can easily lead to ennui, such that "life swings like a pendulum to and fro between pain and boredom."[8]

Our situation is tragic but not altogether hopeless, according to Schopenhauer. In certain types of disinterested contemplation, especially of art and music, the mind briefly escapes the tyranny of the will. Art "stops the wheel of time," and when we manage to transcend our individuality and our will in such acts of aesthetic contemplation, we shall find peace. According to Schopenhauer, the renunciation of individuality and of the will is in effect the central teaching of several great religions, including Christianity, and the most important truth is that "it would be better for us not to exist."[9] Suicide, however, would be a philosophical mistake. He claimed that any genuine denial of the will-to-live would involve shunning life's pleasures, whereas a suicidal person merely wants to escape its sorrows.

A wise person who sees through the veil of worldly illusion will become an ascetic and embrace chastity, poverty, fasting, and even self-torture. Schopenhauer himself did not embrace any of these things. He settled for the consolations of art and music as a way to transcend individuality. His daily flute practice was followed by a lunch so large that it prompted amazement and anecdotes in the Frankfurt restaurant where he ate every day.

Wittgenstein told friends that as a teenager he had not known what to make of Schopenhauer's notion of the world as will. But he wrote about the will and other topics in a Schopenhauerian way in his philosophical notebooks when he was in his late twenties: "It would be possible to say (à la Schopenhauer): It is not the world of Idea that is good or evil, but the willing subject."[10] In these notebooks and in his *Tractatus*, which grew out of them, he often used Schopenhauer's language or imagery to explore the relation between the self and the world, the nature of value, timelessness, and other philosophical matters.

Gretl Wittgenstein, who was rereading Schopenhauer just before Ludwig completed the *Tractatus*, noted down a speculation about science and philosophy. Soon it will be shown, she wrote, that electromagnetism and the vital energy of living things are in fact the same force, and "Schopenhauer's will and Einstein's energy . . . will be unified." Science and philosophy, she continued, will thus have arrived at the same truth from different directions. Schopenhauer himself had unconvincingly claimed in 1836 that his philosophy "received corroboration in all its principal points from the empirical sciences."[11] But he maintained the traditional view that philosophy had its own distinctive job to do, and that science would not supplant it.

By the middle of the nineteenth century, however, the empirical sciences were marching into the territory of philosophy, especially in Germany. Advances in physiology and experimental psychology, among other things, and the spread of Darwinian ideas after the publication of *The Origin of Species* in 1859, seemed to bring the nature of mind, the nature of life, and the question of man's place in the universe into the purview of natural science. What was left for philosophy? A particularly influential set of reflections on this question by Emil du Bois-Reymond, one of the most prominent scientists in Germany in the late nineteenth century, were discussed in the Wittgenstein household. Du Bois-Reymond characterized science as "the resolution of natural processes into the mechanics of atoms." He argued that we ought to confess ignorance about large questions that cannot be addressed by this method, such as the explanation of consciousness, the ultimate nature of matter, and the freedom of the will. These riddles lie beyond the limits of our knowledge, according to du Bois-Reymond. This suggested to some people that philosophy might as well give up trying to solve them. A few scientists went further: they claimed that if the methods of science cannot answer a question, then the question does not even make sense. Thus Ludwig Büchner, a doctor and scientist, announced in a materialist treatise published in 1855 that any account of philosophical subjects "which cannot be brought into harmony with the results of the natural sciences is a jumble of words without meaning."[12]

In late 1903, just when the teenage Ludwig started school, a public lecture in Vienna about science and philosophy got a rapturous reception from a crowd so large that there was a dangerous crush in the hall, according to the newspapers. The lecture was the first in a series given by a distinguished and entertaining physicist, Ludwig Boltzmann, who became something of a celebrity and was granted an audience with the emperor. Wittgenstein came to know of Boltzmann's work while he was at school and apparently expressed a wish to study physics with him. Boltzmann was far from enthusiastic about philosophy: the *Neue Freie Presse*, summarizing the first lecture, noted that he had developed an aversion to it.[13] But he was enthusiastic about aircraft, which may have been what stimulated Ludwig's early interest in them.

Ludwig read a volume of Boltzmann's popular talks and essays that included a lecture entitled "On a Thesis of Schopenhauer's." Boltzmann began by stating that its title was to have been "Proof That Schopenhauer Is a Stupid, Ignorant Philosophaster, Scribbling Nonsense and Dispensing Hollow Verbiage That Fundamentally and Forever Rots People's Brains." The immoderate language was Schopenhauer's own: as Boltzmann pointed out, these words were merely what Schopenhauer himself had written about another philosopher, Hegel. Boltzmann criticized Schopenhauer and his ilk for, among other things, inappropriately seeking to establish some scientific matters a priori—that is, in advance of empirical evidence or experiments. One example was the number of spatial dimensions. Schopenhauer, echoing Kant, reasoned that there must be exactly three of them. Boltzmann replied that there was no "must" about it, and that according to the latest mathematics, there might well be more. He also attacked Schopenhauer's loose use of the term *will* and his overgeneralized arguments about the human condition. Happiness depended on individuals and their circumstances, according to Boltzmann. No unhappy person was helped if we "give him metaphysical proof that life itself is a disaster. If, however, we are looking for means to heal or alleviate physical or moral weakness, we can at least actually help some unhappy people." All in all, it seemed to Boltzmann that "just as Schopenhauer's ideas have shown themselves to be untenable, so too are those of all other philosophers in their central core."[14]

In another lecture, "On Statistical Mechanics," Boltzmann was more conciliatory. If philosophy would learn to collaborate with empirical science on topics that lie on "the border region between philosophy and physics," then real progress was possible. One central task of a reformed philosophy would be to determine exactly which questions were genuine and which apparent puzzles consisted merely of a confused "overshooting the mark on the part of our thinking habits." As Boltzmann put it in some of his lecture notes, "We have to stop asking questions which make no sense." Such questions include: "What is the cause that everything must have a cause . . . ? Do only I myself, only man, or only mammals, or even stones have consciousness? Is God outside or inside this world?" Unlike du Bois-Reymond, Boltzmann did not think that such riddles lie beyond our narrow understanding, but rather that they are illusory, just as Hertz had claimed that some apparent puzzles about force and electricity are confusions that somehow arise from our use of language. Ernst Mach, another Viennese physicist whose popular writings Ludwig knew, had argued the same. "Every *real* problem can and will be solved in due course," wrote Mach. The apparently unanswerable ones are "wrongly formulated and . . . therefore not problems at all." According to Boltzmann, if philosophy could help to extinguish our desire to ask defective questions, it "would become worthy of the name of queen of the sciences."[15]

In 1894, nine years before his celebrated series of lectures on science and philosophy, Boltzmann gave a talk on aeronautics in which he predicted that airplanes would prove to be superior to airships—that is, to self-propelled steerable balloons. But there were great challenges ahead: the inventor who overcame them would have to be "not only a genius, but also a hero." Only someone with "the courage to trust his life to the new element and the cunning to overcome gradually all its treacheries has a chance to kill the dragon which, until this very day, deprives mankind of the treasures of this invention."[16] In Boltzmann's opinion, hardly any other problem was so alluring. This talk was reprinted in the collection that Ludwig read, and perhaps his later study of aeronautics was a sally against Boltzmann's dragon. Similarly, Ludwig's work in philosophy may be seen as an attempt to rise to another of Boltzmann's challenges, that of vanquishing its illusory questions.

Boltzmann suffered from depression and killed himself at the age of sixty-two in September 1906, a few months after Ludwig left school. Even if Boltzmann had still been alive, Ludwig would not have been able to study under him. Graduation from his type of school, which was a *Realschule*, rather than the more academic *Gymnasium* attended by Paul, did not qualify him for admission to a university. But it did qualify him for the sort of institution that his father had attended some four decades earlier, a technical high school, of which the best in the German-speaking world was considered to be Berlin's. Ludwig registered there as a student of mechanical engineering in October 1906 and lodged with the family of one of his professors, a mathematician. Gretl was living in Berlin at the time; she had moved there in 1905 with her husband, who worked at a chemical institute. Berlin was also where their late brother Rudi had lived as a student of chemistry until his suicide in 1904.

Unlike his father, who had left Vienna's technical high school empty-handed, Ludwig emerged from Berlin with a leaving certificate, having taken courses in physics, chemistry, mathematics, mechanics, and several branches of engineering. Little else is known about his three semesters in Berlin, except that he often went to the opera, and that it was during his Berlin years that he began his lifelong habit of noting down thoughts about himself.

His Berlin notebooks are lost, but some later autobiographical reflections list ten people whose lines of thinking Ludwig describes himself as having "passionately" taken up: in addition to Schopenhauer and Boltzmann, the list includes two writers who made their first impacts on him either when he was at school or when he was in Berlin. They are Karl Kraus (1874–1936), the satirist and journalist who had lampooned Karl Wittgenstein, among many other targets, when Ludwig was a child, and Otto Weininger, author of *Sex and Character*, an overheated fusion of biology, psychology, and philosophy. (Ludwig seems to have been more interested in what Weininger wrote about character than in what he wrote about sex.) Weininger's book appeared in June 1903. Four months later, he achieved celebrity at the age of twenty-three, albeit posthumously, when he shot himself in the house where Beethoven had died. A tombstone inscription written by Weininger's father reads: "When he had delivered the message of his soul, he could no longer remain among the living. He betook himself to the place of death of one of the greatest of all men . . . and there destroyed his mortal body."[17]

The dead Weininger and the living Kraus were among the most controversial figures in Vienna during Ludwig's teen years. Weininger was notorious for the positions he defended, of which more shortly. Kraus was notorious for what he attacked, which was more or less everything. Stefan Zweig called him "the master of poisonous mockery." Kraus did his mocking mainly in the 922 issues of *Die Fackel* (the *Torch*), a periodical he founded in 1899 and to which he was the sole contributor in its last twenty-five years of publication, from 1911 to 1936. He announced in its first issue that it aimed to drain "the vast swamp of slogans and clichés." Kraus used journalism to assail journalism. He especially loathed the politically and commercially corrupt Viennese newspapers, believing that the press as a whole had a corrosive effect on culture. Newspapers were only part of a wider problem. Kraus felt himself to be living at a time when language itself was in a state of decay.[18] High art and low commerce, elevated literature and muckraking journalism had somehow become muddled in a Viennese mélange.

Ideologies were mostly confused, and ideas tended to be bad, or so it would seem from the way Kraus wrote about them. New ones were particularly suspect—psychoanalysis, for instance, was "the mental disorder for which it takes itself to be the cure." The providers and consumers of psychoanalysis were mostly Jewish, and another aphorism of Kraus's read simply: "They have the press, they have the stock market, and now they have the unconscious as well."[19] Since this was Vienna, there was no need to spell out who "they" were.

Kraus was not exactly antisemitic, more anti-everything.

He wrote that "my hatred of the Jewish press is exceeded only by my hatred of the antisemitic press, while on the other hand my hatred of the antisemitic press is exceeded only by my hatred of the Jewish press."[20] His religious affiliations were similarly evenhanded. Born into a Jewish family, he believed that all Jews ought to assimilate, and formally renounced membership of Vienna's Jewish community in 1899. Twelve years later, he joined the Catholic Church, despite having ridiculed Catholicism, especially for its illiberal sexual ethics. Then, after twelve years as a Catholic, Kraus left the church, lambasting it for, among other things, blessing bombs.

It was not only the cultural and religious institutions of Austria that Kraus found alien, but the spirit of a technological age that had moved too fast for its own good. "We were complicated enough to build the machine," Kraus wrote in 1908, "and we are too primitive to put it to our service. We are operating a world-wide system of communication on narrow-gauge lines of thought." As a result, he complained in one of his tirades, the printing press, cars, and telephones brought only "the mass-dissemination of mindlessness."[21]

Kraus had a "seemingly unlimited capacity for moral indignation," as one historian of Vienna put it. Ludwig made a similar impression. He "always made a moral issue of everything," according to a Cambridge friend in whose house he stayed for a while in 1929. Ludwig was such a keen reader of *Die Fackel* that he had it sent to his refuge in Norway when he was working there alone in 1913–14, and a few years later, seeking to publish his *Tractatus*, he sent the manuscript first to Kraus's publisher, telling a close friend, Paul Engelmann, an architect who knew Kraus, that he was keen to know what Kraus thought of it. But although Ludwig evidently admired him and sympathized with many of his disaffected stances, he did not say how Kraus had influenced him, except in matters of style: Kraus was a superb "architect of sentences" whose aphoristic manner of expression he sought to emulate. In later life, Ludwig came to think that both of them had taken aphorizing too far, a criticism he expressed rather aphoristically: "Raisins may be the best part of a cake; but a bag of raisins is not better than a cake."[22]

Engelmann saw parallels between the *Tractatus* and Kraus's work, as he explained in a memoir written after Ludwig's death. Kraus had been exercised by "the journalistic practice of mixing news with comment and the falsification of genuine ideas by cliches," Engelmann wrote, while Ludwig's *Tractatus* was directed against "the mingling of the sciences with metaphysics." The aim of the *Tractatus* was to "draw a clear line between what can and what cannot be said," as Engelmann put it, and thus to mark out the limits of language. One of Kraus's aphorisms had mentioned bumping up against "the wall of language" and recoiling from it with a bloody head. Ludwig seems to have liked this image. In a talk he gave in 1929, he spoke of the futile urge to "run against the boundaries of language" when addressing questions of religion or ethics. And in later work, he wrote of "the bumps that the understanding has got by running up against the limits of language."[23]

Englemann invoked Kraus to elucidate a gnomic remark in the *Tractatus:* "Ethics and aesthetics are one." According to Engelmann, it was a key theme of Kraus's—and also of Weininger's—that "the morality of an artist is vital to his work." A book ought to be judged not only by impersonal aesthetic criteria, but also with reference to the author's character as it is manifested in the book. Ludwig was inclined to see literary and philosophical works in this way. If an author was lacking in self-knowledge, or was not a decent soul, or did not write from the heart, Ludwig would be sure to draw attention to this fact. Kraus's hostility to the press must also have struck a chord, since Ludwig always used "journalist" as a term of abuse. In a letter to his former landlady in Berlin, he professed repugnance at her "unnatural and—forgive me the word—journalistic ways of expressing yourself."

At Cambridge, he told a student who planned to distribute notes of his lectures that he would prefer to resign if his teaching could not be kept "clean, & free from a connection with journalism." Ludwig had a broad conception of what counted as journalism: he once wrote to a friend that "Einstein is just a bloody journalist," apparently objecting to Einstein's public statements about disarmament and other nonscientific matters.[24]

Like Kraus, Weininger was born into a Viennese Jewish family, converted to Christianity, and rued the decline of culture and the "machine-like march" of science. Unlike Kraus, he bluntly stated exactly what was to blame for the ills of modern times: "Our age is not only the most Jewish, but also the most effeminate of all ages," he wrote in *Sex and Character*.[25]

According to Weininger, each person is a mixture of masculine and feminine traits: morality, clear thinking, originality, and genius are masculine; childishness, vanity, the lack of a true self, and a fixation on biological reproduction are feminine. The fact that the world had become too feminine and that it had become too Jewish were related problems because Jewishness is "steeped in femininity." The book's table of contents is a menu of provocations: "Prospects of the women's movement. Its fundamental error . . . The soullessness of Woman . . . Radical difference between male and female mental life . . . The Jew lacks genius . . . Christianity and Judaism as the ultimate opposites . . . The effemination of Man."[26]

Sex and Character was based on Weininger's doctoral dissertation about sexuality, an early version of which he showed to Freud, who seems to have been somewhat encouraging, though he annoyed Weininger by telling him that he ought to provide more proof of his ideas. In a footnote to one of his case studies, Freud summarily diagnosed Weininger as "sexually disturbed." On another occasion, he said of their one meeting, "I could not help feeling that I stood in front of a personality with a touch of the genius." Freud also noted "a veiled, quite beautiful look in his eyes," though Weininger's fellow student at Vienna University, Stefan Zweig, said he always looked as if he had just emerged from a thirty-hour train journey. A sort of vogue for Weininger lasted for several decades after his death. The novelist Elias Canetti wrote that some young men he knew in Vienna in the 1920s "indulged in the arrogance of higher literature: if not Karl Kraus, then Otto Weininger or Schopenhauer. Pessimistic or misogynous utterances were especially popular, even though none of these boys was a misogynist or misanthrope."[27]

James Joyce and Gertrude Stein were among the many writers who were at least somewhat taken by Weininger's book. A few, including the dramatist August Strindberg, greatly admired its account of the sexes: "To see the woman problem solved is a deliverance for me," Strindberg wrote to Weininger. But it was not necessary to share Weininger's views in order to be intrigued by them. Some readers were both fascinated and repelled. A review in a Munich journal called Weininger's account of female psychology monstrously brutal, yet added that "one must, must, must read this book."[28]

Ludwig apparently agreed. For three decades, he recommended Weininger's writings to his family, friends, pupils, and colleagues—sometimes *Sex and Character*, sometimes a posthumously published collection of Weininger's essays and aphorisms, *On Last Things*. During Ludwig's military service, his sister Hermine wrote to him that she was much enjoying some Weininger he had commended to her: "It replaces you a bit."[29] He received a very different reaction fifteen years later when he urged *Sex and Character* on his friend G. E. Moore, who was a professor of philosophy at Cambridge. Moore seems to have found the book full of fantasy, to which Ludwig replied that this was true, but that Weininger was nevertheless great: "It isn't necessary or rather not possible to agree with him but the greatness lies in that with which we disagree. It is his enormous mistake which is great. I.e. roughly speaking if you just add a '~' [a negation sign] to the whole book it says an important truth. However we better talk about it when I come back."[30]

If Ludwig did discuss the matter further with Moore, there is no record of what was said. And the few passing references to Weininger in Ludwig's writings shed no light on what this "important truth" may have been. Perhaps the point of his evasive joke about negation was that Weininger was at least asking the right questions, or in some way thinking in the right terms, even if he did not always arrive at the right answers. Ludwig did once explicitly disavow Weininger's main thesis, according to a conversation reported by a ponderous acolyte, Maurice Drury:

> DRURY: Weininger seems to me to be full of prejudices, for instance his extreme adulation of Wagner.
>
> WITTGENSTEIN: Yes, he is full of prejudices, only a young man would be so prejudiced.
>
> And then with regard to Weininger's theme that women and the female element in men was the source of all evil he exclaimed: "How wrong he was, my God he was wrong."[31]

Ludwig evidently did not think that Weininger was wrong about everything: on several topics, Weininger's opinions matched views or attitudes that Ludwig later expressed. It is, however, impossible to say what in Weininger influenced him and what he liked because he had already had a similar thought himself.

One summer evening in 1919, when Ludwig was a prisoner of war, he read aloud to others from an essay by Weininger about Ibsen's *Peer Gynt*, in which Weininger stated that the "deepest problem of ethics" is "truth and the lie." Peer Gynt, wrote Weininger, "wants to get away from the lying which is indissolubly connected to life—no one is so holy that he has not seen himself forced over and over again into a white lie, and the white lie is as morally inexcusable as any other." Ludwig's desire to purge himself of untruthfulness or insincerity was uncompromising. It is what his distant relative the economist Friedrich Hayek noticed about him on their first meeting, on a night train to Vienna in 1918: "What struck me most in this conversation was a radical passion for truthfulness in everything." Hayek remarked that this was characteristic of certain young Viennese men at the time: "One had to 'live' truth and not tolerate any pretence in oneself or others. It sometimes produced outright rudeness and, certainly, unpleasantness." Perhaps growing up in the Wittgenstein household helped to form Ludwig's sometimes awkward penchant for veracity. His brother Paul was similarly unwilling to utter anything but the blunt truth. Paul told an interviewer that he did not hide his disappointment when Ravel first played him the piano concerto he had commissioned because "I had never learned to pretend."[32]

One dictum in *Sex and Character* could have served as Ludwig's motto: "*Truthfulness, purity, fidelity, sincerity toward oneself:* that is the only conceivable ethic. There are only duties to oneself." Of artists and thinkers, Weininger wrote, "The greater they are, the more ruthlessly they keep faith with themselves" and "The truly exceptional individual, no matter what he is thinking about, is basically only thinking about himself." Weininger was not criticizing such self-absorption but admiring it. Ludwig, too, regarded introspection as an ethical imperative: "*Far* the most important thing," he wrote to Russell in 1913, "is to come to terms with myself!" Gretl once said that the only career befitting a member of the Wittgenstein family was to be a reformer of some kind; Ludwig wanted only to reform himself. He expressed disapproval of his sister's urge to go and help others whenever she heard of some unfortunate event in the wider world.[33]

Hermann Broch, a Viennese novelist and critic who was a contemporary of Ludwig's, described Weininger as "the most passionate ethical thinker since Kant." Weininger presented his strongest and strangest views as the ineluctable conclusions of moral arguments, which (unlike Kant) he followed to the edge of fanaticism and beyond. Weininger judged sexual intercourse to be so morally abhorrent that he advocated universal chastity and countenanced the extinction of humanity. According to him, men and women use sexual partners solely as a means to an end, either to produce a child or to satisfy lust, which violated Kant's supreme ethical maxim that one must never use a person purely as an instrument. To perpetuate mankind would therefore be "to perpetuate a problem and a guilt." It was time to end what he called "the whole modern *copulation culture*," for which women were primarily to blame.[34]

Weininger claimed that *Sex and Character* is "not about women but about Woman." That is, it is concerned with femininity in the abstract, or "*absolute* Woman." Although he heaped insults on the soulless absolute Woman, Weininger professed to be a champion of actual women: they "are *human beings* and must be treated *as such*, even if they themselves would *never* want this." Men and women have equal rights, he proclaimed, though he added that it would be unwise to permit women any share of political power "for the time being and possibly forever."

His discussion of Jews played a similar game. Weininger claimed that his target was not actual Jews—who must not be persecuted—but rather "the Jew," or Jewishness in the abstract, which is a set of qualities, or "cast of mind," that can be exemplified by people of any race or religion, though its most striking manifestation is to be found in "historical Judaism." This cast of mind is marked by "an eternal wandering back and forth before the gate of reality," which makes the absolute Jew duplicitous, avaricious, and a coward, with no self, no soul, and no real belief in anything. Some non-Jews share these qualities and may even be "more Jewish than many Jews." Even Richard Wagner, who was in Weininger's eyes the "most profound of anti-semites" as well as the greatest of artists, "cannot be cleared of having a Jewish element," because his music is sometimes flashy and too loud.[35]

Weininger wrote that the Jew "does not sing," "totally lacks . . . pride in his ancestors," and is "humourless." Perhaps he had never been to a service in a synagogue or met a descendant of a famous rabbi or heard a Jewish joke. Since he was supposedly writing about an abstraction, Weininger presumably felt free to ignore facts about actual Jews. But he did not stick to his story. Weininger wove back and forth between remarks about Jewishness in his abstract sense and remarks about "the Jewish race"—which he thought was probably related to "the Negro," because Jews have "readily curling hair." And he often referred approvingly to the writings of straightforwardly antisemitic writers, such as Houston Stewart Chamberlain, an unhinged English polymath who purported to believe that even the wealthiest Jews chose to live among vermin.[36]

According to Weininger, a "Jewish materialistic type of science" that was hostile to all philosophy had unfortunately become dominant. He wrote that Jews are inclined to a mechanistic outlook that leaves no room for anything transcendent, whereas "the Aryan perceives the striving to understand and explain *everything* as a devaluation of the world, because he feels that it is precisely the unfathomable that gives existence its value. The Jew has no respect for mysteries, because he does not sense any anywhere."[37] Weininger complained that the patrons of culture used to value artists and philosophers, but now focus instead on science and technology: "Laboratories and seminars admirably perform the functions of the capitalist barons of industry." True culture is on the wane, and "the voice of the culture-wolf howling for popularized natural science, presses very audibly on the listener's ear."[38]

Strip out the talk of Aryans and Jews, and Ludwig's feelings about science, philosophy, and culture were similar to these attitudes of Weininger's. In the early 1930s, Ludwig wrote, "The dreadful thing about the scientific way of thinking (which possesses the whole world today), [is] that it wants to answer every disquiet with an explanation." And in his *Tractatus*, he contrasted the ancients, who left room for mystery by invoking an inexplicable God or Fate, with the inferior modern view of the world, which "makes it appear as though *everything* were explained." The fact that scientists rather than artists were the idols of the age distressed him, and a "superficial curiosity about the latest discoveries of science" was one of the "lowest desires of modern people," as he put it in a lecture in 1929. Twenty years later, Ludwig told a friend, "This is the age of popular science, and so this cannot be the age of philosophy."[39]

Ludwig had a fondness for suggestive generalizations based on vague notions of type. Weininger provided plenty of food for such thoughts. One of Weininger's essays, which Kraus published in *Die Fackel*, divided people into two categories: "seekers," those who search for the truth and are vain, sensitive, and introspective (Brahms and Dürer were said to be examples), and "priests," those who robustly preach the truths they have learned (Shelley and Handel). Ludwig particularly liked a fragmentary essay of Weininger's that described parallels between human psychological types and various species of animals. In later life, he sometimes classified his Cambridge friends according to Weininger's zoological typology. Ludwig was also stimulated by the synoptic formulas of Oswald Spengler's *The Decline of the West*. The book was factually unreliable, Ludwig conceded, but "Spengler does point out certain very interesting comparisons."[40]

Although he never attributed any of modernity's shortcomings to the influence of Jews, Ludwig did believe various unflattering generalizations about them. His remarks about Jews and Jewishness were relatively mild by the standards of his family, but nonetheless blinkered. The following is a notebook entry from 1926 by his sister Hermine:

> Paul vehemently maintains that dishonesty lies deep in every Jew.
>
> Ludwig drew my attention to the fact that by living in foreign states, under foreign laws, circumstances, and constraints, Jews have become unnatural creatures. Perhaps the two are connected.
>
> I believe that the Aryan and Jewish races are diametrically opposed in their merits and deficiencies, at least in Europe, and are bound to be in conflict either openly or covertly. . . .
>
> I also believe that it must be very difficult for the Jews, even if they have a high and a deep insight, like [Paul] Engelmann, to see clearly. Can one be an Austrian and a Jew, or *really* only one of them?[41]

Weininger wrote of "the perennial limitations of the purely Jewish mind." Breathing the miasma of Viennese antisemitism made some people question themselves even if they had only traces of Jewish ancestry. For example, Hugo von Hofmannsthal, a Viennese writer who was fifteen years older than Ludwig, had just one Jewish-born grandparent, but worried in his youth that a few "Jewish drops of blood" were affecting his mind. Ludwig expressed similar thoughts about himself. In 1931, when he was lecturing at Cambridge, he wrote in a notebook,

> The saint is the only Jewish "genius." Even the greatest Jewish thinker is no more than talented. (Myself for instance.)

> I think there is some truth in my idea that I am really only reproductive in my thinking.[42]

Ludwig also noted that it is "typical of the Jewish mind to understand someone else's work better than he understands it himself." The notion that Jews are intellectually skilled but incapable of original thought was almost a commonplace in Vienna. A popular saying had it that "science" (or sometimes "literature" or "culture") is "what one Jew copies from another."[43]

In his forties, Ludwig several times mulled over "the Jew" and "the Jewish mind" in his private writings. The "semitic races" have an "*unpoetic* mentality." There is "something Jewish" about Rousseau. Mendelssohn, a "reproductive" artist, was "perhaps the most untragic of composers" because tragedy is "unjewish." One must beware of confusing "the nature of a Jewish work with that of a non-Jewish work." And the Jews have recently given the world nothing that deserves "warm *gratitude*," he wrote in 1937. Ludwig made observations about the idea that Jews have a "secretive and cunning nature" and "their liking to be rich" without ever questioning such stereotypes.[44]

Before the rise of Nazism, Bertrand Russell employed Jewish stereotypes in a handful of letters to fellow members of the British upper classes. A psychologist he met was "not the sort of man I could ever like because of the touch of Jew vulgarity," he wrote in 1914 to Lady Ottoline Morrell. But Russell came to see the error of his ways. In an article for *Reader's Digest* in 1941 he warned: "If you are at a party where someone begins to disparage the Jews, or any other race, do not let them get away with it. Remember that it is from such small beginnings that terrible persecutions grow. . . . If you share such a prejudice, struggle against it."[45]

A few pages later on in the notebook in which Ludwig wrote that he was merely a reproductive thinker, he tentatively qualified this remark. Perhaps he had once given birth to "new lines of thinking," in 1913–14, when he was working on questions about logic that had first seized his imagination as an engineering student in Manchester. When he turned fifty, Ludwig again probed his own creativeness, this time expressing his self-doubts in terms of a distinction between originality of the seed and originality of the soil. Perhaps he had no seed of his own, he wrote, but "sow a seed in my soil, & it will grow differently than it would in any other soil."[46] It does seem true that what he gleaned from his reading often grew into something very much his own.

The choice of Manchester as the place for Ludwig to continue his engineering studies was a wise one and probably his father's. The science and technology at its university were internationally renowned, and the city had a large community of Germans who had been drawn there in the second half of the nineteenth century by Manchester's precocious industry. The place was, as a local music critic put it, "good for a young man to live in during the years before the 1914–1918 war. The Germans had given the place a solid culture; they came to Manchester for trade and brought their music with them."[47]

When Ludwig first arrived in the summer of 1908, shortly after his nineteenth birthday, he lived at an inn on the moors east of Manchester and conducted experiments with box kites at the university's nearby upper-atmosphere research station. He was unnecessarily cold in his room, as he later recounted to a friend in Cambridge, because "he was unused to landladies and to the English, and it never occurred to him that he could ask for more coal."[48] He befriended a fellow engineering student who was staying at the inn, William Eccles, who recalled that Ludwig's wealthy background was evident, though not ostentatiously displayed. When they wanted to take a trip to the seaside at Blackpool, Ludwig proposed to hire a special train to take them there.

Other reminiscences of Ludwig at this time mentioned his "outstanding" natural charm and courtesy, and his immaculate attire. Eccles's wife remembered that he was "something of a favourite with the ladies." But he was no smooth gentleman when at work. After experimenting with kites and balloons, Ludwig progressed to aeroengines: a colleague recalled that "he was doing some work on combustion of gases and his nervous temperament made him the last person to tackle such research, for when things went wrong, which often occurred, he would throw his arms about, stamp around and swear volubly in German." After one particularly trying day at work, he went to a concert by Manchester's symphony orchestra and its Austrian conductor, Hans Richter, a leading interpreter of Brahms and Wagner. This "restored my equanimity entirely," Ludwig wrote to Hermine.[49]

Swearing, stamping, and tinkering with equipment led to an invention for which Ludwig successfully sought a patent in his second year at Manchester, a complicated type of propeller jet that was somewhat analogous to a Catherine wheel firework. According to the patent application, it consisted of a "radially armed motor each arm carrying a combustion chamber, and exhaust nozzle at its extremity and each arm formed as a, or fitted with, a propeller blade." There was at the time no practical way to make this contraption work, but thirty-five years later something similar was briefly used in a type of helicopter.[50]

Ludwig had already made another sort of discovery in his first year at Manchester: Bertrand Russell's *The Principles of Mathematics*, which had been published in 1903. Reading this book was the beginning of the end of his life as an engineer.

The book proposed an answer to the question: What sort of truths are mathematical truths? Russell argued that they were logical truths. A logical truth is usually described by philosophers as a statement that is necessarily true because of its form or structure. Thus, "If all cows have six legs, and Mabel is a cow, then Mabel has six legs" is a logical truth. It does not matter that cows do not in fact have six legs, and it would not matter if Mabel were not a cow; it must still be true that if cows had six legs and Mabel were a cow, then she would have six legs.

Russell aimed to show that a few concepts of logic were enough to provide definitions of all the concepts of pure mathematics, and that the truths of pure mathematics could be deduced from a handful of logical principles. A later three-volume work,

Principia Mathematica, which Russell wrote together with his former teacher A. N. Whitehead, laid out these deductions in detail—it arduously arrived at "1 + 1 = 2" on page 83 of its second volume, and cracked a joke while doing so. *The Principles of Mathematics* laid some of the philosophical groundwork for these deductions. This involved investigations not only of mathematical and physical concepts, including infinite wholes, classes, measurement, continuity, series, dimensions, motion, and causality, but also concepts used in logic, including implication, variables, and denotation. There is a chapter on proper names, adjectives, and verbs, which Russell acknowledged might at first seem irrelevant to his topic; but he maintained that what he called "philosophical grammar" sheds light on logic and on many other philosophical matters.[51]

There are two appendices to the book that seem particularly to have caught Ludwig's eye. The first explained and praised the work of a German mathematician and philosopher, Gottlob Frege (1848–1925), who was in those days little known, but whose contribution to logic is now reckoned as second only to Aristotle's. Frege and Russell had worked independently to reach similar conclusions, though Frege maintained only that arithmetic, not all of pure mathematics, could be reduced to logic. Russell wrote in this appendix that Frege's work "abounds in subtle distinctions, and avoids all the usual fallacies which beset writers on Logic."[52] Ludwig made a pilgrimage to meet Frege in the summer of 1911, his third year at Manchester, and continued to study and admire Frege's writings for the rest of his life. He had some of Frege's works decoratively bound by the Wiener Werkstätte, a collective of craftsmen whose most dazzling production, a vitrine of almost two hundred pounds of silver, jewels, and glass, sat in the Palais Wittgenstein.

The second appendix to Russell's *Principles* proposed a tentative solution to a puzzle, now known as Russell's paradox, which he had found in his analysis of classes. The puzzle concerns what Russell once aptly called "a very peculiar class"—the class of all classes that are not members of themselves. The problem posed by this class may be illustrated by a roughly analogous puzzle involving a very peculiar barber, whom Russell described as "one who shaves all those, and those only, who do not shave themselves." Does this barber shave himself? If he does, then he doesn't. And if he doesn't, then he does—in which case, he doesn't, and so on. The same sort of contradictory loop may be generated by asking if the class of all classes that are not members of themselves is a member of itself. The barber version of the puzzle is easy to solve: the answer is that there can be no such barber. But the notion of a class is intertwined with other logical notions in a way that makes it hard to explain how there can fail to be a class of all classes that are not members of themselves. Russell's paradox left him feeling that he did not really know what a class is. Frege was aghast when Russell informed him of the problem. He wrote back that Russell's discovery "has surprised me beyond words and, I should almost like to say, left me thunderstruck, because it has rocked the ground on which I meant to build arithmetic."[53]

Russell mooted an ad hoc "theory of types" to solve his paradox. He postulated a hierarchy of types of objects, and stipulated that statements are to be counted as meaningless if they mingle elements from different levels of the hierarchy in the wrong way. The idea was to rule out oddities such as the class of all classes that are not members of themselves. But Russell was uneasy about his makeshift theory of types, and ended his book with a confession and an invitation: "What the complete solution of the difficulty may be, I have not succeeded in discovering; but as it affects the very foundations of reasoning, I earnestly commend the study of it to the attention of all students of logic."[54]

Ludwig, rising to this challenge during his first year at Manchester, proposed an answer to the paradox, which he sent to a British mathematician, Philip Jourdain. There is no record of exactly what this answer was. Two and a half years later, Ludwig, still pondering such matters, went to Cambridge to talk to Russell, apparently at Frege's suggestion. He talked so much that at first Russell found him a bore. But Russell soon came to regard Ludwig's appearance as a "great event in my life—whatever may become of him."[55]

4

The Next Big Step

When Wittgenstein appeared in Cambridge in October 1911, Russell was a thirty-nine-year-old lecturer whose notable achievements had been in logic and philosophy but who had also become active in public life. His parents died young, and he was brought up by his paternal grandmother in a house given to his grandfather by Queen Victoria. This grandfather was twice prime minister and had visited Napoleon on Elba. Like Wittgenstein, Russell was schooled mostly at home. Also like Wittgenstein, he felt somewhat obliged to emulate his impressive family, which in Russell's case had been prominent in politics since the early sixteenth century.

After finishing *The Principles of Mathematics* in 1902, Russell had labored on the mathematical logic of *Principia Mathematica* for a decade, often for ten hours a day. He also stood unsuccessfully for Parliament, campaigned for women's suffrage and free trade, and published several philosophical essays. He was immersed in a love affair with a fellow aristocrat, Lady Ottoline Morrell, when Wittgenstein arrived. Russell's stream of letters to her provides a running commentary on the drama of Wittgenstein.

Something about him intrigued Russell at once. "I am much interested . . . and shall hope to see a lot of him," he wrote to Morrell at the end of Wittgenstein's first day. By the next evening, it was already evident that this young pupil was not going to sit quietly at Russell's feet: Wittgenstein "threatens to be an infliction—he came back with me after my lecture and argued until dinner time—obstinate and perverse, but I think not stupid." A fortnight later, Russell seemed to be losing his patience: "My . . . engineer, I think, is a fool. He thinks nothing empirical is knowable—I asked him to admit that there was not a rhinoceros in the room, but he wouldn't."[1]

After another fortnight of turbulent discussions, Russell reported that Wittgenstein "is armour-plated against all assaults of reasoning—it is really rather a waste of time talking to him." But a few weeks later, he was coming to like him: "He is literary, very musical, pleasant-mannered (being an Austrian), and I *think* really intelligent." Wittgenstein could not decide whether or not to abandon engineering, and wanted to know if he was any good at philosophy, so Russell asked him to write something during his Christmas holidays in Vienna. The verdict on his homework was positive: "I shall certainly encourage him," Russell wrote to Morrell in January 1912. "Perhaps he will do great things. On the other hand I think it very likely he will get tired of philosophy."[2] Wittgenstein continued to be taxing and sometimes a bore, but there was no more talk of him being a fool.

The Christmas holidays of 1911 seem to have been a turning point for Wittgenstein. In the summer of 1912, he told his new close friend David Pinsent that for the past nine years until the previous Christmas he had felt "de trop in this world." Coming to Cambridge to study under Russell had been his "salvation." It was probably during these same holidays in Vienna that Wittgenstein had a sort of mystical experience, which he continued to recount almost four decades later. He attended a musical peasant comedy by a popular Austrian writer, Ludwig Anzengruber, in which a miserable road-mender lies down in a field and is suddenly suffused with a happy feeling: "Nothing can happen to you!" For Stefan Zweig, this saying, which became proverbial in Viennese dialect, captured the "eternal gay unconcern of old Vienna." To Freud, it represented an impulsive flouting of danger. But to Wittgenstein it expressed a transcendent assurance that external events cannot harm one's inner self—an "experience of absolute safety," as he put it in a public talk in 1929. Seeing the play, he told a friend, was what first showed him "the possibility of religion."[3] This may be the only known instance of a noted thinker receiving enlightenment from a musical comedy.

Wittgenstein was admitted to Trinity, Russell's Cambridge college, in February 1912 and quickly made his mark. In March, Russell pronounced him a genius, and G. E. Moore (then a lecturer and also at Trinity) told Russell that he "always feels Wittgenstein *must* be right when they disagree." Russell was at this stage so taken with his pupil that he indulgently glossed Wittgenstein's harsh directness as an admirable lack of "the false politeness that interferes with truth." Wittgenstein had found his place in the world, at least for now: "He said the happiest hours of his life had been passed in my room," Russell wrote to Morrell.[4] Sometimes when he came to argue about logic, Wittgenstein brought him roses. Russell hoped that his college servant would assume that flowers sent by Morrell had also been from Wittgenstein, which would have helped to conceal their affair. Morrell was married and Russell was separated; their involvement could have cost him his job at Trinity.

* * *

Russell had been wearied by his work on *Principia Mathematica* and felt that Wittgenstein would "solve the problems I am too old to solve." The twenty-two-year-old had "more passion about philosophy than I have," Russell told Morrell. "He says every morning he begins his work with hope, and every evening he ends in despair—he has just the sort of rage when he can't understand things that I have." As well as expressing impatience with himself, Wittgenstein was unsparing in his criticism of others. He let Russell know that he hated his latest book, and he scolded Moore for his "very bad" lectures on psychology. (Psychology was then treated in Cambridge as part of philosophy.) Wittgenstein had never properly studied logic, so Russell sent him to be tutored by W. E. Johnson, a senior Cambridge philosopher who wrote a textbook on the subject. Johnson soon politely ended the arrangement, as his pupil would not listen—he talked only about his own ideas. Wittgenstein said he realized in the first hour that Johnson "had nothing to teach me."[5]

But Johnson was devoted to music, a point strongly in his favor. Wittgenstein remained fond of him for many years and made discreet arrangements to supplement his small income. Music accompanied several of Wittgenstein's Cambridge relationships: his regular visits to Moore, who sang and played piano, often included music-making à la Wittgenstein. Wittgenstein also performed his classical whistling with Pinsent, an easygoing mathematics undergraduate and pianist who had an interest in philosophy. The two friends developed a repertoire of some forty Schubert songs, and often went to concerts. For a while in 1912 they also went to Cambridge's newly established psychology laboratory, where Wittgenstein conducted experiments on the perception of rhythm with Pinsent as his guinea pig.

Pinsent kept a diary that recorded, among other things, Wittgenstein's struggles and triumphs during their times together in Cambridge and on two holidays abroad. His account of Wittgenstein's work is admiring, though vague, and, when they first met, rather amused: "He is reading philosophy up here, but has only just started systematic reading: and he expresses the most naïve surprise that all the philosophers, he once worshipped in ignorance, are after all stupid and dishonest and make disgusting mistakes!"[6] Wittgenstein's triumphs, according to Pinsent, included a "system . . . which is wonderfully simple and ingenious and seems to clear up everything." It seemed to Pinsent that "the mucky morass of Philosophy is at last crystallising about a rigid theory of Logic—the only portion of Philosophy about which there is any possibility of man knowing anything." Wittgenstein's work had overturned some of Russell's, Pinsent noted, but "Russell would be the last to resent that, and . . . it is obvious that Wittgenstein is one of Russell's disciples and owes enormously to him."[7]

There were also distressing setbacks to report. On holiday in Norway in September 1913, Pinsent recorded that Wittgenstein had been depressed all day about work, and "is morbidly afraid he may die before he has put the Theory of Types to rights." Six months earlier, Wittgenstein had twice resorted to hypnosis in the hope that revelations about logic could be extracted from his unconscious while he was in a trance. He often found it hard to capture his thoughts. And even when he did manage to express his conclusions, Wittgenstein was unable or unwilling to explain how he had reached them. "I told him he ought not simply to *state* what he thinks is true, but to give arguments for it," Russell wrote to Morrell, "but he said arguments spoil its beauty, and that he would feel as if he was dirtying a flower with muddy hands."[8]

The flowers that Wittgenstein was attempting delicately to arrange were the foundations of logic. While Russell aimed to explain mathematical truth in terms of logical truth, Wittgenstein dug deeper into logical truth itself. What do the symbols used in *Principia Mathematica* really amount to? He found this an entrancing topic. "There is nothing more wonderful in the world than the *true* problems of Philosophy," he wrote to Russell in a letter about the logical symbols for "and," "or," and "if—, then—."[9]

"Logic must turn out to be of a TOTALLY different kind than any other science," Wittgenstein wrote to Russell in the summer of 1912. This conviction put him somewhat at odds with both Russell and Frege. Consider the logical truths expressed by formulas such as "Either P or not-P" or "If P and Q, then P." These locutions strip the flesh from ordinary language and display its logical bones; they hold true no matter which statements are substituted for "P" and "Q." But what exactly are these skeletal truths about? For Russell, logic was "concerned with the real world just as truly as zoology, though with its more abstract and general features." Frege saw it as a science that studies the laws of truth. But Wittgenstein came to think that propositions of logic are not about anything. As he later put it in his *Tractatus*, they represent "the scaffolding of the world" and have no subject matter of their own. According to him, the truths of logic display the logical properties of our language—that is, they show what follows from what—by combining propositions that say something informative (such as "It is Monday") to form propositions that "say nothing" (such as "Either it is Monday or it is not Monday"). He called these truths of logic "tautologies," a term that was usually employed merely to denote superfluous repetition—Johnson's book on logic, for example, mentioned "the sin of tautology."[10] For Wittgenstein, logical truths were empty, but they were empty in an interesting way. His development of this idea was an advance on Frege's and Russell's somewhat nebulous thoughts on the subject.

A decade before Wittgenstein came to Cambridge, Russell had arrived at the opinion that good philosophy depends on a sound analysis of propositions. He was convinced of this by studying the seventeenth-century polymath Leibniz, not because Leibniz advocated such analysis but because his philosophy illustrated the folly of neglecting it. According to Russell, Leibniz had been driven to fanciful theories about the world by the dogma that every truth can be expressed as a proposition with a subject and a predicate. In one way or another, many bad ideas in philosophy stemmed from faulty ideas about propositions, or so Russell maintained. This was rather an oversimplification in the case of Leibniz, and perhaps generally, but the notion was a stimulating one and was embraced by Wittgenstein.

Wittgenstein's first publication, a scornful review of a traditionalist logic book, championed the new symbolic logic that had been devised by Frege, Russell, and Whitehead. This logic replaced the old subject-predicate format with more flexible concepts borrowed from mathematics, and had other merits. Wittgenstein compared recent progress in logic to the leaps that "made Astronomy out of Astrology, and Chemistry out of Alchemy." In his *Tractatus*, he gave the credit for one such leap to Russell, who had shown that the grammatical form of a proposition may disguise its logical properties.[11]

Wittgenstein was thinking primarily of the "Theory of Descriptions," which Russell proposed in order to deal with—among other things—assertions about nonexistent objects, such as "The present King of France is bald." The theory recast this proposition so that instead of predicating "is bald" of a subject, "the present King of France," it was taken to assert the existence of a single object with two properties, that of being king of France and that of being bald. On Russell's analysis, since there is no object that possesses the property of being king of France, the assertion is as straightforwardly false as it would be if there were a king of France and he had plenty of hair. According to Russell, this analysis helps to make it less of a mystery that we can formulate meaningful assertions about nonexistent

Bertrand Russell in 1914

things. Looking back at the theory four decades later in his *History of Western Philosophy*, Russell proudly claimed that it "clears up two millennia of muddle-headedness" about existence.[12]

Wittgenstein admired and had great affection for Russell, but there were personal differences that ran deep. One clash emerged in early 1912 when Russell published *The Problems of Philosophy*, which appeared in the Home University Library, a series of short introductions to academic subjects. Writing to his editor, Russell referred to it as "my treatise on philosophy for your shop-assistants." He did not bother the shop assistants with too many points about propositions and logic, but dealt mainly with questions about knowledge, which he once described to Morrell as "the most essentially philosophical of all questions."

(Russell's desire to reduce mathematics to logic was motivated partly by his wish to explain how mathematics is knowable.) The treatise began with a challenge: "Is there any knowledge in the world which is so certain that no reasonable man could doubt it?"[13] Russell then examined various sorts of knowledge, and the kinds of things of which we are generally thought to have it, and ended with two chapters about the nature and benefits of philosophical inquiry. It was these remarks at the end of the book that seem particularly to have annoyed Wittgenstein, though he may have had other objections as well.

"What he disliked about my last chapter," Russell wrote to Morrell, "was saying philosophy has *value;* he says people who like philosophy will pursue it, and others won't, and there's an end of it. *His* strongest impulse is philosophy." This may seem a small matter about which to get cross, but it evidently touched a nerve for Wittgenstein: a similar issue contributed to a worse explosion two years later. Wittgenstein had been mulling their relationship, he wrote to Russell from Norway in 1914, and found "enormous differences in our natures," of which the only example he gave—though he said there were others—was their contrasting attitudes to "the value of an intellectual work." So there could not be any real friendship between them, according to Wittgenstein. Although he would be grateful to Russell "and devoted to you WITH ALL MY HEART for the whole of my life, . . . I shall not write to you again and you will not see me again either."[14] Wittgenstein later relented, as he often did after an eruption.

The value of philosophy, Russell had argued in *The Problems of Philosophy*, lies mainly in the questions that it asks. It rarely gives answers that can be known to be true, but it is the uncertainty of philosophical inquiry which makes it valuable. Anyone untouched by philosophy, Russell wrote, goes through life imprisoned in prejudices. The questions of philosophy thus expand our conception of what is possible, stimulate the imagination, and diminish dogmatism. Russell finished the book with a lofty flourish, echoing a passage in Plato to the effect that speculative contemplation can lead the mind toward "that union with the universe which constitutes its highest good."[15] Russell's writings of this period sometimes sounded the spiritual tone that he knew Morrell wanted to hear from him.

According to Russell, philosophy begins where science ends. This is not because philosophy yields some higher form of knowledge, but because it examines questions that science does not yet know how to address. He once put it that "science is what you more or less know and philosophy is what you do not know." It follows that the border between philosophy and science may shift as more becomes known. Russell observed that this fact largely explains why philosophy seems to have made little progress: "As soon as definite knowledge concerning any subject becomes possible, this subject ceases to be called philosophy." He mentioned astronomy and psychology as examples of territories that had once been parts of philosophy but later won independence as sciences in their own right. The same thing happened to logic during Russell's lifetime. Four decades after *The Problems of Philosophy*, he noted that recent advances in logic had solved "what *were* philosophical problems."[16]

A certain type of fundamental probing is the only thing that distinguishes philosophical from scientific inquiry, Russell wrote in *The Problems of Philosophy*. Philosophy "examines critically the principles employed in science and in daily life; it searches out any inconsistencies . . . in these principles, and it only accepts them when . . . no reason for rejecting them has appeared." Wittgenstein may at this stage have had a similar conception of philosophy, according to the official record of a four-minute talk he gave in 1912 in which he defined philosophy as "all those primitive propositions which are assumed as true without proof by the various sciences."[17] But while Russell liked to stress affinities between science and philosophy, Wittgenstein came increasingly to insist on the differences.

In his later work, after he returned to Cambridge in 1929, Wittgenstein lamented that "philosophers constantly see the method of science before their eyes, and are irresistibly tempted to ask and answer questions in the way science does. This tendency . . . leads the philosopher into complete darkness."[18] Russell thought it led to the light. He believed that philosophers would do well to cultivate the "instinct of scientific caution" and to imitate the piecemeal and collaborative working practices of scientists.[19]

Wittgenstein "abominates ethics and morals generally," Russell told Morrell when reporting Wittgenstein's denial that there was anything objectively valuable about philosophy. The subject came up again a few months later when the two men were discussing some eighteenth-century love letters: "I asked him how he would feel if he were married to a woman he loved and she ran away with another man. He said (and I believe him), that he would feel no rage or hate, only utter misery. His nature is good through and through; that is why he doesn't see the need of morals. . . . His outlook is very free; principles and such things seem to him nonsense, because his impulses are strong and never shameful."[20]

Russell's generous talk of unfailingly noble impulses would have been rejected by Wittgenstein, who took a dimmer view of his own character. One bad evening, Wittgenstein expressed "the most piteous disgust with himself," Pinsent recorded on one of their holidays.[21] But Russell was correct that Wittgenstein rejected moral principles, at least in one sense of the term. Wittgenstein regarded values as personal and particular: the right thing to do was not a matter for general rules that applied in all circumstances or for all people. As Desmond Lee, one of Wittgenstein's pupils in 1929–31, noted in a memoir: "I do not remember him making any general pronouncements on morals; but . . . his views on particular situations were often strong and definite, and he had a passionate moral seriousness which expressed itself in everything he did rather than in particular precept."[22] An ethical judgment is "a personal act," Wittgenstein once wrote, not "a statement of fact." In his *Tractatus*, he claimed that "it is clear that ethics cannot be put into words." This is because language, as he then conceived it, can express only what lies within the realm of fact, whereas values "must lie outside the whole sphere of what happens and is the case."[23]

Wittgenstein later changed his conception of language—it had been too narrow—but not his conception of values. They remained somehow a personal matter. His friend Rush Rhees remarked that Wittgenstein "would emphasize that one man's nature and another's are not the same, and that what is right (or imperative) for one man may not be right for another." Given such a stance, one might expect him to have refrained from judging others, and indeed Lee found that he was "not in the least censorious." But more people found the opposite. One thing that made it always taxing to be with Wittgenstein, according to his friend and former pupil Norman Malcolm, was his "tendency to be censorious." Wittgenstein may in theory have been speaking only for himself when he delivered his verdicts on matters of taste and on how one should live. But to his hearers, it must often have felt as if they were being reprimanded (which, in practice, they sometimes were). Georg von Wright, one of his literary executors, recalled that every conversation with Wittgenstein "was like living through the day of judgment. It was terrible."[24]

One such day of judgment came in November 1912 when Russell and Wittgenstein walked by the river Cam and watched a boat race. Russell recounted to Morrell that the fierce competition between rowers disgusted Wittgenstein, bringing on a tirade:

> He suddenly stood still and explained that the way we had spent the afternoon was so vile that we ought not to live, or

> at least he ought not, that nothing is tolerable except producing great works or enjoying those of others, that he has accomplished nothing and never will, etc.—all this with a force that nearly knocks one down.
>
> He makes me feel like a bleating lambkin.[25]

Wittgenstein was fragile at the time. Ten days earlier, Russell reported that his pupil had been "on the verge of a nervous breakdown, not far removed from suicide. . . . Whatever he says he apologises for having said. He has fits of dizziness and can't work—the doctor says it is all nerves."[26] Russell suggested riding, among other practical measures, and Morrell sent some cocoa tablets for Wittgenstein to take. But making headway with the problems of logic was the only remedy that distracted Wittgenstein from the problems of himself. When he had progress to report, all was suddenly well for a while. A few days after the outburst on the riverbank, Russell berated Wittgenstein for thinking too much about himself, and he threatened to stop listening unless Wittgenstein became desperate. Perhaps Wittgenstein's anxiety was magnified by Russell's great expectations of him, which had been announced to his sister Hermine earlier that year. On the other hand, Wittgenstein might have been in an even worse state without Russell as his champion.

Russell had introduced Wittgenstein to some of his non-philosopher friends from the Bloomsbury literary set and from the partly overlapping circle of Cambridge's semi-secret discussion club, the Apostles. "Everyone has just begun to discover Wittgenstein; they all now realize that he has genius," Russell told Morrell. One impressed new friend was John Maynard Keynes the economist, who lobbied for Wittgenstein's admission to the Apostles. Wittgenstein was elected in November—unlike Pinsent, who had also been considered—but soon stopped going to the meetings. He found the younger members immature, though it was two of the older ones, James and Lytton

Strachey, who referred to him behind his back as "Herr Sinckel-Winckel" and "the Witter-Gitter man."[27] Wittgenstein's friendship with the well-connected Keynes proved to be a lasting one. Keynes gave him aid and counsel in practical matters over many years, from spiriting the manuscript of the *Tractatus* out of an internment camp in Italy in 1919 to helping Wittgenstein obtain British citizenship twenty years later.

Karl Wittgenstein was dying when Ludwig went to Vienna for the holidays in December 1912. He had "the most beautiful death that I can imagine . . . falling asleep like a child," Ludwig wrote to Russell in January. He had not felt sad in his father's last hours, "but most joyful and I think that this death was worth a whole life."[28] When Wittgenstein returned to Cambridge, Pinsent recorded the impression that it was Karl or his long illness that had kept Wittgenstein back. No doubt Pinsent had been told the same as Russell: that Karl wanted this son to be an engineer or businessman. But it was not all plain sailing once Karl was out of the way. Wittgenstein continued for much of his life to struggle in his philosophical work and to be doubtful about the wisdom of doing it. If Karl held him back, then he continued to do so from the grave.

Later that year, Pinsent noted that although Wittgenstein had been very fond of his father, he "can't stand most of his family." In all likelihood this is an example of how easy it was to misinterpret Wittgenstein's conversation. It is true that he, like Hermine and probably others of the siblings, could not stand Gretl's unbalanced and domineering husband, Jerome Stonborough, an American of German Jewish background who later killed himself. And there were tensions and rows with Paul and Gretl. But Wittgenstein was deeply attached to his family, however much he complained about them. He was habitually vehement, volatile, and unguarded, and because he inspired a kind of awe, his throwaway remarks were not always thrown away. Thus

Pinsent also recorded a conversation about votes for women: "He is very much against it—for no particular reason except that 'all the women he knows are such idiots.'" Wittgenstein certainly had old-fashioned attitudes to the sexes. In later life, according to Rhees, he stated that even if there were plenty of great women composers, "this would not make me think more highly of women. What I'd admire in any woman would be . . . something I'd never expect or look for in a man." Several people noted his apparent dislike of intellectual women and his initial hostility to having women in his Cambridge classes. But his prejudice was far from entrenched. There were quite a few women among his chosen inner circle of pupils, and he picked his close friend Elizabeth Anscombe to be the translator of his second book, *Philosophical Investigations.* One pupil, Georg Kreisl, quoted him as saying that "men are foul, but women are viler."[29] It is plausible that Wittgenstein uttered these words, but not that he meant them.

Wittgenstein's working relationship with Russell changed during 1913: "I find I no longer talk to him about *my* work, but only about his," Russell complained in April. Wittgenstein's self-centered style of debate was noted by many people. It was captured especially well in the diary of a fourteen-year-old boy whose family he visited in 1942: "He's an impossible person everytime you say anything he says 'No No, that's not the point.' It probably isn't his point, but it is ours." What annoyed Russell in 1913 was not just that Wittgenstein increasingly commandeered the agenda for their talks but that his aggressive manner inhibited the constructive cooperation Russell wanted philosophy to copy from science. He "treats infant theories with a ferocity which they can only endure when they are grown up," Russell told Morrell.[30] The next month, when Russell showed him parts of a book he was writing, Wittgenstein strangled it in its crib. At first, Russell could not understand Wittgenstein's criticisms, but he suspected they were just. He left the book unfinished.

Wittgenstein's attack was aimed at Russell's analysis of statements about what someone believes (or hopes or denies or doubts), such as "Othello believes that Desdemona loves Cassio." According to Wittgenstein, Russell's theory had the defect of being unable to distinguish sense from nonsense. In particular, it could not explain why "Othello believes that Desdemona loves Cassio" does make sense, but "Othello believes that the table penholders the book"—to adapt an example of Wittgenstein's—does not. The records of Wittgenstein's objection are cryptic; attempts to reconstruct its details continue to this day.[31] One thing that is clear is that Russell felt paralyzed by it for a while, though he was partly fishing for sympathy when he later told Morrell, during a crisis in their romance, that the episode had convinced him that his days of doing fundamental work in philosophy were over.

Wittgenstein's objection was part of a larger train of thought. He was coming to believe that a proper logical symbolism, if only one could find it, would automatically eliminate nonsense of various kinds by making it impossible to express in the symbolism. (There would then be no need to make arbitrary stipulations such as the theory of types in order to deal with Russell's paradox.) Similarly, a proper logical analysis of belief would somehow make it clear that Othello cannot be said to believe that a table penholders a book. In order to develop a proper theory of logical symbolism and analysis, what was needed was "a correct theory of propositions," as Wittgenstein put it to Russell.[32] In order to find such a theory, it emerged that Wittgenstein would need to go off and work on his own.

The plan to leave Cambridge and be alone with logic emerged during a holiday in Norway with Pinsent in September 1913. They spent most of the trip at a hotel in the village of Öystese, about fifty miles east of Bergen, where they hired a sailing boat and went about with it on a fjord—"or rather Pinsent is doing all the sailing and I sit in the boat and work," Wittgenstein wrote to Russell. Wittgenstein toiled on the theory of types while Pinsent, when not required to sail, studied Roman law. In the evenings, they played dominoes and performed Schubert songs, as usual without any singing. Wittgenstein became sulky on their first day in Norway and again on their first day in Öystese, but the equable Pinsent was well suited to coping with such squalls. It was clear that Wittgenstein was "quite incapable of helping these fits," for which he was very contrite afterward. Pinsent calmly regarded him as just "different from other people—he is if anything a bit mad." Besides, he was "a very charming companion so long as friction is avoided."[33]

Wittgenstein's moods upset Pinsent less than they upset Wittgenstein himself. One reason he came up with his plan to live a hermit's life, which he announced toward the end of the holiday, was to achieve the sort of greatness that could lift the stain of being such a difficult person: "He feels that he has no right to live in . . . a world where he perpetually finds himself feeling contempt for others, and irritating others by his nervous temperament—without some justification for that contempt *etc*, such as being a really great man and having done really great work."[34] Cambridge was full of distractions and interruptions, Wittgenstein told Pinsent, and there was much still to be done. Unless he "absolutely settles all the foundations of Logic," his work would be of little use to the world, and time was running out.[35] For no apparent reason, Wittgenstein felt he would not live much longer. As soon as he and Pinsent arrived back in England, some family news added to the urgency of the matter. Gretl and her impossible husband were about to move to Oxfordshire, and Wittgenstein did not want to be subjected to visits from them.

In case he expired before making further progress, Wittgenstein felt he must explain his latest ideas to Russell before beginning his retreat. He read out some thoughts from his notebooks, which were "as good as anything that has ever been done in logic," Russell told Morrell. Russell urged him to write out his ideas more fully, but Wittgenstein could not manage it. The perfectionism of his "artistic temperament" got in the way, according to Russell.[36] So notes were taken by two secretaries and by Russell while Wittgenstein held forth over a number of days in early October.

Wittgenstein then put his possessions into storage and went back to Norway in mid-October, settling in Skjolden, a lakeside village north of Bergen. Thus ended his unorthodox two-year spell as a philosophy student. He had gained no formal qualifications but had obtained acknowledgment from a partly congenial English elite that he was the genius he felt he needed to be. Wittgenstein intended to return to Cambridge once he had managed to write something, though in fact he stayed away for fifteen years. "Our acquaintance has been chaotic but I have been very thankful for it: I am sure he has also," Pinsent wrote in his diary when they parted. Russell was worried that Wittgenstein would not survive his solitude, since he would have nothing with which to divert himself when work went badly. "I expect he will commit suicide towards the end of winter," Russell wrote to Morrell, "but it can't be helped. He has done *admirable* work."[37]

Sometimes Russell's enthusiasm for an apparently marvelous mind was revised after a while. When he first knew D. H. Lawrence in 1915, he told Morrell that he "sees everything and is always right." Four decades later, Russell wrote that in retrospect he did not think Lawrence's ideas "had any merit whatever." In the case of Wittgenstein, Russell came to think that he had followed him too blindly in the early days; and he never liked his later philosophy of the 1930s and 1940s. But he always acknowledged that Wittgenstein's first work "had an almost incredible degree of passionately intense penetration."[38]

* * *

Wittgenstein's life in Skjolden was not entirely eremitical: he made several friends among the locals and started to learn Norwegian. "I have got two nice rooms here in the Postmaster's house and am looked after very well indeed," he wrote to Russell after two weeks in Norway. He seems to have secured just the right amount of solitude, regarding his circumstances as ideal for work, though it was still hard to catch his ideas while they were in flight: "All sorts of new logical stuff seems to be growing in me, but I can't yet write about it."[39]

Russell had questions about the work that Wittgenstein had dictated in England, and what he had managed to convey in letters, but these queries were not always welcome. Wittgenstein had a violent dislike of explaining himself: "It is INTOLERABLE for me, to repeat a written explanation which even the first time I gave only with the *utmost repugnance*." His thoughts about logic and language were still delicate flowers that required gentle handling. Their arrangement was, however, taking shape in a promising way, especially his exploration of the idea that logical truths are empty tautologies. Was there a means of displaying the formulas of logic so that one could distinguish the vacuously true ones (tautologies) from the vacuously false ones (contradictions) just by looking at them on the page? The challenge of creating such a system of symbols or diagrams was "the fundamental problem of logic!" Wittgenstein excitedly wrote to Russell. But it was all distressingly hard, as he explained to him in mid-December. "My day passes between logic, whistling, going for walks, and being depressed. I wish to God that I were more intelligent and everything would finally become clear to me—or else that I needn't live much longer!"[40]

It seems that logic was too engrossing for him to go back to Vienna for an important family event on 1 December. Paul Wittgenstein was to have his debut as a concert pianist, for which he had hired an orchestra and Vienna's main concert venue, its "Golden Hall." A year after their father's death, both Paul and Ludwig were making progress in their uncommercial callings. "Overjoyed at your marvellous success, which one hears everywhere," wrote one of Paul's Figdor cousins, enclosing a gift of a Mendelssohn manuscript from his enormous collection of artistic treasures.[41] A review of Paul's debut in the *Neue Freie Presse* was brief yet encouraging—not as much of a boost as being hailed by Bertrand Russell as the next big thing in philosophy, but a good start.

Wittgenstein spent about a fortnight with his family in Vienna over Christmas, during which time he alternated between apathy and the feeling that he would go mad. "I keep on hoping that things will come to an eruption once and for all, so that I can turn into a different person," he wrote to Russell from the Palais.[42] The opportunity for such a transformation arrived seven months later when war broke out.

"My life has been one nasty mess so far," Wittgenstein wrote to Russell in March 1914, when he briefly proposed to end contact between them. Although they both had faults, Wittgenstein explained, his own were worse. His existence was "FULL of the ugliest and pettiest thoughts and actions imaginable (this is *not* an exaggeration)."[43] But he was hopeful that things would improve for him. He was looking forward to a visit from Moore at Easter, and proposed another summer holiday with Pinsent. On balance, a relatively isolated existence in Skjolden suited him well, so he planned to have a retreat built for himself in the area. A small, two-story house was constructed just over a mile from Skjolden, perched above a lake, though Wittgenstein did not stay in it until after the war.

In April, Wittgenstein dictated his latest thoughts to Moore, whom he had collected in Bergen and escorted to Skjolden. The dictation began with what Wittgenstein later described as the "main contention" of his *Tractatus*, that there are things that can be shown but not said:

> Logical so-called propositions *show* [the] logical properties of language and therefore of [the] Universe, but *say* nothing.
>
> This means that by merely looking at them you can *see* these properties; whereas, in a proposition proper, you cannot see what is true by looking at it.
>
> It is impossible to *say* what these properties are, because in order to do so, you would need a language, which hadn't got the properties in question.[44]

In this dictation, Wittgenstein confined his contrast between showing and saying to matters of logic. But by the time of his *Tractatus*, he had found broader uses for it. Most notably, he claimed that what philosophers had tried to say about ethics and the meaning of life lay in the realm of what shows itself, but cannot be said: "There is indeed the inexpressible. This *shows* itself; it is the mystical." Philosophers had been trying to say the unsayable. Hence the *Tractatus*'s famous concluding injunction: "Whereof one cannot speak, thereof one must be silent."[45]

In his music-obsessed family, with a mother whose thoughts flowed only at the piano, Wittgenstein grew up on a diet of the verbally inexpressible. The works of Beethoven and others provided daily reminders of the greatness beyond words. Some remarks that Wittgenstein made about people and about books suggest that he most esteemed what was manifested discreetly rather than paraded openly or explicitly stated. His sister Hermine's many virtues were modestly veiled, "as human qualities *should* be." He wrote to a friend that Tolstoy impressed him far more when he just told a story instead of addressing the reader directly: "His philosophy is most true when it's *latent* in the story." And discussing a "really magnificent" poem by Ludwig Uhland with his friend Paul Engelmann in 1917, Wittgenstein wrote: "This is how it is: if only you do not try to utter what is unutterable then *nothing* gets lost. But the unutterable will be—unutterably—*contained* in what has been uttered!"[46]

When Moore arrived back in Cambridge in late April 1914, he made inquiries about a bachelor's degree for Wittgenstein, who apparently wanted to submit a piece of writing about logic as a dissertation. Moore reported back that the regulations required such an essay to include notes detailing the candidate's sources. Wittgenstein was enraged that such "STUPID *details*" could apply in his case, and more or less told Moore to go to hell.[47] Wittgenstein somewhat relented two months later, writing to Moore that he hoped they could still be friends. But Moore was so upset that he did not want to see Wittgenstein again, and there was no contact between them for the next fifteen years.

Pinsent, however, did want to see Wittgenstein again, despite initial misgivings about their planned third holiday, which he confided to his diary: "Last September, when he was so terribly difficult to get on with, I remember swearing to myself that never again would I go on a holiday alone with him."[48] The plan was to meet in London in late August and proceed somewhere from there. Pinsent suggested Scotland as a sensible option, since the recent murder of the Emperor Franz Joseph's heir made it likely that there would be hostilities in continental Europe. The trip was called off when Austria-Hungary declared war on Serbia on 28 July. Wittgenstein was exempted from military obligations because of a double hernia, but he told Pinsent that he was not allowed to leave Austria. His brother Paul was a reserve officer in the Dragoons and joined his regiment four days after the declaration of war. Kurt, the third surviving Wittgenstein brother, was a reserve officer in the same cavalry regiment, but had moved to New York to work in the steel industry three months earlier. He was apparently prevented from returning to fight until April 1917, when the United States ended its neutrality in the war.

Ludwig decided to volunteer for military service one week after Paul, and was sent untrained to an artillery regiment in Kraków two days later. "I feel an absolute conviction that he will not survive—he is reckless and blind and ill," Russell wrote to Morrell. But if he does survive, Russell added, "I think the war will have done him good." That was what Wittgenstein hoped. Another of their Cambridge circle, Ferenc Békássy, who had been elected to the Apostles in the same year as Wittgenstein, had similar hopes for himself. "I am sure to get something good out of the war unless I die in it. It's part of the 'good life' just now, that *I* should go: and the sooner one gives up the idea that the *world* can be better than it is, the better," Békássy wrote to Nöel Olivier, an English beauty with whom several Apostles, including the poet Rupert Brooke, were in love.[49] (Békássy was killed four days after arriving at the front; Wittgenstein got to know Nöel Olivier three decades later when he fell in love with her son.)

According to Hermine, Ludwig joined the Austrian army not only to defend his country but because he had "an intense wish to take on something difficult" and to do nonintellectual work. Two years earlier, Russell and Wittgenstein had been discussing how not to lose one's soul: Russell thought "it depended on having a large purpose that one is true to," but Wittgenstein said it depended more on "suffering and the power to endure it." In this respect, Wittgenstein's war did not disappoint. It provided challenges that "saved my life; I don't know what I would have done without it," he told one of his nephews. On his first deployment, aboard a boat on the eastern front in 1914, he wrote in his notebook that because the Russians were close, he would have "the opportunity to be a decent human being, for I'm standing face to face with death." But transformation was slower to arrive than he had expected. Twenty months later, on the eve of a dangerous assignment, Wittgenstein was still hoping that the war could "at last begin for me. And maybe life, too! Perhaps the nearness of death will bring light into my life."[50]

Russell, meanwhile, campaigned against the war. He was not in principle opposed to all wars. But "this flaming death of our civilisation and our hopes," he wrote in a letter to the *Nation* in August 1914, "has been brought about because a set of official gentlemen, living luxurious lives, mostly stupid, and all without imagination or heart, have chosen that it should occur rather than that any one of them should suffer some infinitesimal rebuff to his country's pride."[51] Unlike Békássy, Russell believed that the world could be made better than it is. His efforts to achieve this by agitating against the war brought him repeatedly into conflict with British authorities. In 1916, he was prosecuted and fined for a leaflet objecting to the treatment of a conscientious objector, which led the council of Trinity College to dismiss him from his lectureship. When Harvard University offered him a post, the British Foreign Office prevented him from leaving the country to take it up. In 1918, he was prosecuted for a second time under the Defence of the Realm Act and sentenced to six months in prison, though in comfortable conditions that allowed him to write an *Introduction to Mathematical Philosophy* and other things.

In this *Introduction*, Russell gave credit to Wittgenstein for showing him the significance of tautologies, noting that he did not know whether Wittgenstein had made further progress on the matter "or even whether he is alive or dead."[52] The last time he had heard from him was almost three years earlier, in October 1915, when Wittgenstein wrote from an artillery workshop train in what is now Ukraine. Russell heard nothing more until February 1919, by which time Wittgenstein was himself a prisoner, in Italy, and had finally succeeded in assembling his philosophical thoughts into a treatise that he was eager to publish.

Wittgenstein's treatise (later called the *Tractatus*) was compiled largely from remarks he had written in diary-like notebooks throughout the war, including when he was at the front. During periods of leave, and maybe when on quieter assignments, these fragmentary thoughts were pruned, polished, and threaded together with the aid of a decimal numbering system that is superficially similar to the one used in *Principia Mathematica.* (All but 7 of its 526 numbered remarks are structured as a cascading hierarchy of comments on other numbered remarks.) In later life, Wittgenstein wanted the notebooks to be destroyed, but some survived by chance. They show that he was engaged in three struggles at once during the war. There was a military struggle, a philosophical struggle, and a spiritual one. Military life appears in the notebooks mostly in the form of discomforts and frustrations rather than heroics, though Wittgenstein was in fact decorated for bravery at least four times, including for his actions during a famously bloody Russian offensive in 1916. A notable fact about his philosophical struggle is that he worked with at least as much dedication and profit in repugnant circumstances during wartime as he had done in tranquil Norway under circumstances that he had regarded as ideal. His spiritual anguish is registered in the notebooks alongside his daily activities and philosophical ideas: "From time to time I become an *animal.* Then I can think of nothing but eating, drinking, sleeping. Dreadful! And then I also suffer like an animal, with no possibility of inner salvation."[53]

Wittgenstein's literary executors silently excised all but his philosophical remarks when they published these notebooks. One can almost sympathize: it feels indecent to peer over Wittgenstein's shoulder at his sometimes bluntly intimate private records and despairing imprecations to God. The censored passages were mostly written in a very simple code. Some years later, Wittgenstein noted what a strange sort of relief it was "to write down some things in a secret script which I would not like to have written legibly."[54]

In his first days in the army, Wittgenstein recorded in his moderately secret code that his fellow soldiers were swinish, crude, stupid, malicious rogues. Sustained exposure to the common man did not mellow his attitude: two years later, the men were still mean, heartless, bigoted scoundrels, and he felt himself to be "exiled among utter worms." Wittgenstein later claimed that the war had changed him enormously, but it did not soften his view of humanity. In 1921, when he was a schoolteacher in rural Austria, he wrote to Russell that he was "surrounded, as ever, by odiousness and baseness."[55]

Some solace was provided in wartime by Tolstoy's *Gospel in Brief*, which Wittgenstein bought in his first month of military service and carried with him "*always*, like a talisman." "I say Tolstoy's words over and over again in my head: 'Man is powerless in the flesh but free because of the spirit.' May the spirit be in me! . . . God give me strength. Amen. Amen. Amen."[56] Thoughts of Pinsent also brought solace—"Letter from David! I kissed it"—but anxiety as well.[57] He longed for David, wondered if David thought as much about him, and often noted the absence of news from him. Terrible news arrived in July 1918, when Pinsent's mother informed Wittgenstein that David had been killed while flying as a scientific observer over southern England. He had been investigating the causes of stalling in flight as part of his mathematical work at the Royal Aircraft Establishment.

Wittgenstein seems to have been in love with Pinsent, at least in retrospect. There is no sign that Pinsent was aware of such feelings when they were together or that he felt them himself. "Every day I think of Pinsent," Wittgenstein wrote to Russell two years later. "He took half my life away with him." Wittgenstein dedicated the *Tractatus* to David's memory, and wrote to Mrs. Pinsent that it was to David that he owed "far the most part of the happy moods which made it possible for me to work."[58]

When he was with Pinsent, Wittgenstein had been occupied with questions raised by the logic of Russell and Frege. But two years into the war, in August 1916, he noted that his work "has broadened out, from the foundations of logic to the nature of the world." That summer, while he was in great danger on the eastern front, his notebook filled with remarks about good and evil, death, God, happiness, the self, and the meaning of life: "To believe in a God means to see that the facts of the world are not the end of the matter." "I can make myself independent of fate." "Only a man who lives not in time but in the present is happy." "Death is not an event in life. It is not a fact of the world."[59] These stoical and mystical observations, sometimes redolent of Tolstoy's *Gospel* or Schopenhauer, were not entered in code, like his personal remarks and prayers, but written in plain German, like his remarks about technical philosophy.

Wittgenstein's thoughts about logic and about the meaning of human existence were starting to converge. Just as the logical properties of language could be shown but not stated, according to Wittgenstein—that is, they were manifested by our language but could not be described in it—something similar was true of the ethical dimensions of life. The "solution of the problem of life," he wrote in July 1916, "is to be seen in the disappearance of this problem."[60] What he meant is that the problem vanishes because it cannot be stated. In the *Tractatus*, he expanded on this line of thought in the spirit of Boltzmann and Mach:

> 6.5 When the answer cannot be put into words, neither can the question be put into words.
>
> *The riddle* does not exist.
>
> If a question can be framed at all, it is also *possible* to answer it. . . .
>
> 6.52 We feel that even when all *possible* scientific questions have been answered, the problems of life remain completely untouched. Of course, there are then no questions left, and this itself is the answer.

Wittgenstein's notion of a "scientific question" was rather broad at this stage. Every true proposition counted as a scientific one—"The totality of true propositions is the whole of natural science"[61]—and he seems to have regarded "what can be said" and "science" as the same thing:

> 6.53 The correct method in philosophy would really be the following: to say nothing except what can be said, i.e. propositions of natural science—i.e. something that has nothing to do with philosophy—and then, whenever someone else wanted to say something metaphysical, to demonstrate to him that he had failed to give a meaning to certain signs in his propositions. . . . Although it would not be satisfying to the other person . . . *this* method would be the only strictly correct one.

By "metaphysical," Wittgenstein meant philosophical-sounding speculations that stray beyond what can be said. When people blunder beyond the realm of fact into such territory, a good philosopher's job is to shepherd them back to safety by showing that their words do not make sense.

How was that to be done? Wittgenstein's procedure in the *Tractatus* was to develop an account of what it is for a proposition to mean something. One of his main ideas about this came to him in his first months as a soldier: "The proposition *only says something in so far* as it is *a picture!*" he wrote in his notebook in October 1914. Propositions are pictures of reality: to understand one is to "know the situation it represents."[62] The *Tractatus* contains passing observations on many topics, but much of the book elaborates on the idea that meaningful statements are pictures of the world, built up out of "elementary propositions" that can be strung together by logical connectives (such as "and" and "or") to make more complex ones.

Armed with this theory about meaning, Wittgenstein believed that he was in a position to eliminate philosophical problems, which had been posed only because people did not realize how language works and where its limits lie. Once those limits had been established, the job of philosophy was to police them. As he put it in his preface to the *Tractatus:* "The whole sense of the book might be summed up in the following words: what can be said at all can be said clearly, and what we cannot talk about we must pass over in silence."[63]

Wittgenstein more or less completed the *Tractatus* during a period of leave in August 1918, then returned to duty, this time at the Italian front, at the end of September. In November, he was taken prisoner near Trento by the Italians, and put a few finishing touches to his book during nine months of captivity, mostly in Cassino.

The *Tractatus* is an intricate structure in which scholars still wander with delight a century after it was created, even though they know it contains many dead ends. Some of its contributions to logic are enduring; but one notable shortcoming is that it does not accord with its own theory of meaning. For example, according to the *Tractatus*, "Whatever we can describe at all could be other than it is."[64] Science—or "what can be said"—deals with matters of fact, and we can always conceive of such matters as having turned out otherwise, according to Wittgenstein. But what about the descriptions that are to be found in the *Tractatus* itself? Do they describe things that could have been otherwise? Consider a sample of the book's assertions:

4.01	A proposition is a picture of reality.
6.1	The propositions of logic are tautologies.
6.421	Ethics cannot be put into words.
6.4321	God does not reveal himself *in* the world.

If things had been different, could God have revealed himself in the world? Could ethics have been put into words? Might the truths of logic have failed to be tautologies? Might propositions have been something other than pictures of reality? Wittgenstein did not entertain any such possibilities. He recognized that, according to his own theory of meaning, these assertions were meaningless. They purported to describe things that could not have been otherwise, and they also fell foul of his theory in other ways. That is why the book ends up trying to swallow itself:

> 6.54 My propositions serve as elucidations in the following way: anyone who understands me eventually recognizes them as nonsensical, when he has used them—as steps—to climb up beyond them. (He must, so to speak, throw away the ladder after he has climbed up it.)
>
> He must transcend these propositions, and then he will see the world aright.

Did Wittgenstein's disposable ladder of nonsensical propositions enable him to convey something about the unsayable—to contain the "the unutterable" in what is uttered, as he had put it to Engelmann? Most philosophers have been utterly unconvinced. In an introduction that Russell wrote for the *Tractatus*, he lauded Wittgenstein's theory of logic, and the range and profundity of the book, but drily remarked, "What causes hesitation is the fact that, after all, Mr Wittgenstein manages to say a good deal about what cannot be said."[65]

A few thinkers have labored to defend the *Tractatus*'s ladder of supposed nonsense, but Wittgenstein himself simply walked away from it, albeit slowly. In 1930, musing on his changed approach to philosophy, he wrote, "If the place I want to reach could only be climbed up to by a ladder, I would give up trying to get there. For the place to which I really have to go is one that I must actually be at already." He remained sentimentally attached to the *Tractatus* for a long time, despite acknowledging that it contained "grave mistakes," and he used to say that it was "not *all* wrong." But by 1948, according to one of his last pupils,

"We were asked not to read the *Tractatus*, which he regretted not being able to withdraw from circulation."[66]

At the time it was written, though, Wittgenstein deemed the thoughts in the *Tractatus* to be "unassailable and definitive." He believed himself to have "found, on all essential points, the final solution" of the problems of philosophy, as he put it in his preface. "I believe I've solved our problems finally," he wrote to Russell from Cassino in March 1919. "This may sound arrogant but I can't help believing it."[67]

In the closing words of his preface, Wittgenstein made a further claim. If, as he believed, he had disposed of the problems of philosophy, then he had thereby also demonstrated "how little is achieved when these problems are solved." There was, evidently, still the problem of how to live. "I'm not working," he wrote to Hermine from Cassino in June 1919, "and I'm constantly thinking about whether I'll ever be a decent human being and how I am supposed to make that happen."[68] When he was released from captivity two months later, his first steps were to dispose of his fortune and to train as a schoolmaster.

5

Work on Oneself

When Wittgenstein returned from captivity to Vienna in August 1919, he arranged for his money to disappear. He instructed that his portion of the family trusts be redistributed between three of his four surviving siblings, Paul, Hermine, and Helene, thus in effect writing himself out of their father's will. Seven years later, when their mother died, he did the same with an inheritance from her. Russell's impression, after spending a week with Wittgenstein in December 1919, was that he had disinherited himself because "he found earthly possessions a burden."[1]

Even the simple retreat that had been built in Norway was an impediment. Wittgenstein gave the house to the son of the farmer who leased him its land, and thereafter stayed in it as a guest. According to Engelmann, who had become a close confidant, Wittgenstein "shed all the things, big or small, that he felt to be petty or ludicrous," which included his tie as well as his fortune. In his new, unencumbered life, Wittgenstein wore an open-necked shirt, carried around a rucksack with his few things, and continued to sport part of his military uniform until long after the war. This may be why some friends from his Manchester days described him as dressed in "what seemed to be a boy scout uniform" when he visited them in 1925.[2] Perhaps, like his old uniform, the barrack-like austerity of his barely furnished Cambridge rooms in the 1930s and 1940s were a comforting reminder of the years that he thought had saved him.

Tolstoy's *Gospel*, echoing St. Matthew, taught that one should not lay up supplies for oneself on earth. When Russell read a biography of Tolstoy in 1911, a few days before he first met Wittgenstein, he too had been attracted by Tolstoy's "struggles after simplicity." He felt that there was something right about the idea of renouncing the world, or so he wrote to Morrell. This seems to have been a passing fancy, though Russell did over the years give away all or most of his large inheritance. Unlike Wittgenstein, he donated his money to what he regarded as worthy causes, and not in order to unburden himself. Wittgenstein "absolutely refused to put his wealth to any humanitarian purpose," Engelmann recorded, "because he rightly expected that no good would come of it." Engelmann was sure that "a *conscious* resentment of his father or criticism of his business practices played no role . . . whatever" in his decision to rid himself of riches.[3] However, Wittgenstein does seem to have liked the idea of earning his own living, as did Russell.

Until 1919, Wittgenstein had distributed largesse in the family manner. When his father died, he made a substantial donation to Austrian artists and writers because "it is customary in such cases to donate a sum to charitable causes," as he wrote to Ludwig von Ficker, the editor of a literary journal that had been praised by Kraus.[4] Wittgenstein left it to Ficker to distribute the money and to advise on the beneficiaries, who included the poet Rainer Maria Rilke, the architect Adolf Loos, Oskar

Kokoschka, and Ficker's journal itself. During the war, Wittgenstein gave 1 million crowns—ten times as much as his donation to the arts—for the construction of a large mortar that he thought the military needed. It appears that the weapon was never built. According to Hermine, this was one of several ill-conceived donations made by the Wittgenstein children after Karl's death. Ludwig made a more practical gift in 1918 when he sent Frege the money to buy a home for his retirement.

Frege and Ficker were among those to whom Wittgenstein turned for help in finding a publisher. His work in philosophy was over, as he had told friends in Cassino, but he was naturally eager for his treatise to be read. After his return to Austria, more than two years passed before he heard that publication had finally been arranged, during which time he was often desperately miserable. Several times he wrote to Engelmann about his thoughts of suicide. Wittgenstein was usually vague about the causes of his unhappiness—sometimes it was the unspecified "external conditions of my life" or "this filthy world," sometimes "my own baseness and rottenness," and once "the state of *not being able to get over a particular fact*" (perhaps the death of Pinsent).[5] But now and then he openly expressed exasperation about the fate of his book, and was presumably thinking of his underappreciated philosophical work when he wrote to Engelmann in January 1921: "I had a task, did not do it, and now the failure is wrecking my life. I ought to have done something positive with my life, to have become a star in the sky. Instead of which I remained stuck on earth, and now I am gradually fading out."[6]

Just over a year earlier, while Wittgenstein was training to be a teacher, he met with Russell for a week in The Hague. Russell was delighted by their first meeting in six years: "It is a great joy to see him," he wrote to a friend. "He is so full of logic that I can hardly get him to talk about anything personal. He is very affectionate, and if anything a little more sane than before the war." They discussed Wittgenstein's treatise every day, and Russell wrote to Morrell that "I feel sure it is a really great book, though I do not feel sure it is right." He offered to write an introduction to it, which pleased Wittgenstein, who realized that Russell's name would make the book more attractive to publishers.[7]

One firm had wanted Wittgenstein to pay some of the book's costs, which offended his pride. Ficker had said that publishing it in his journal would be financially risky, so Wittgenstein did not press the matter. Frege had been willing to recommend it to an academic journal, but he urged him to make changes that would, in Wittgenstein's opinion, have mangled his precious book. Wittgenstein did not do enough to explain or justify his views, Frege told him. Could he not divide the work into a series of more pellucid and convincing articles?

Wittgenstein's attitude to the comprehensibility of his work was strange. In its preface, he wrote that the book would perhaps be understood "only by someone who has himself already had the thoughts that are expressed in it." He told Russell that he himself found it "all as clear as crystal," but he did little to make it clear to readers: one of its seven principal propositions has a formula containing a symbol that he invented but did not bother to define.[8] It is hard to avoid the conclusion that Wittgenstein was somewhat ambivalent toward being understood by others, though he certainly wanted the treatise published.

A German firm was interested in issuing it together with Russell's preamble, but when Wittgenstein read Russell's introduction in March 1920, he disagreed with much of it, and when he saw its German translation, he could not bear to let it be printed with his book. The prospective publisher therefore withdrew. Wittgenstein wrote to Russell in May that he was comforting himself with the thought that if the book was, like Kant's *Critique of Pure Reason*, a "work of the highest rank," then it made no difference if it was printed now or in a hundred years. And if it was not such a work, then he did not want it to be printed at all.[9]

Russell did not get Wittgenstein's disappointing news for several months, as he had gone to Russia to study the effects of its revolution, which were also disappointing. He met Lenin—"He despises the populace & is an intellectual aristocrat," Russell noted in his diary—and he wrote a book criticizing Bolshevism.[10] When Russell returned to Britain in July 1920, he offered to look for a publisher on Wittgenstein's behalf, and Wittgenstein gave him a free hand.

Wittgenstein had just received his teaching certificate, and had most of two summer months to kill before taking up a school post in the autumn of 1920. His time at a teacher-training college had been somewhat humiliating, since many of the other trainees were boys of eighteen or younger, and he was already thirty. In the eyes of the staff, he also stood out as serious and competent—a model teacher, according to the college's principal. What he now wanted, in his depressed state, was regular work to keep him busy, which he found as an assistant gardener in the plant nurseries of a monastery near Vienna. He worked for eleven hours a day: "When the work is done, I am tired," he wrote to Engelmann, "and then I do not feel unhappy."[11] As a child, Wittgenstein had been uninterested in nature, according to Hermine, but that seems to have changed in adulthood. After his death, the pages of Wittgenstein's philosophical manuscripts were found to contain many pressed flowers.

He had asked to be sent to "the most out-of-the-way school you have," and in late September Wittgenstein began his teaching career in the mountain village of Trattenbach, four hours south of Vienna. This was, surely, the first time that a Trattenbach schoolmaster had written to a professor in Peking, Wittgenstein joked in a letter to Russell, who had just arrived in China to teach there for one academic year. If Russell was lecturing about philosophy, Wittgenstein fondly wrote, "I wish I could attend and could argue with you afterwards."[12] Although he felt that he had no more to contribute to the subject himself, Wittgenstein had evidently not lost interest in philosophy. A month later, he requested copies of some of Frege's works to be sent to Trattenbach.

Russell almost died in China in March 1921. Some obituaries of him were prematurely published in England, where he was newsworthy at the time, not so much for his philosophy but because he was heir presumptive to an earldom. If Russell had succumbed to his pneumonia, the *Tractatus* might have been buried as well, at least for a time. Russell's assistant had in his absence obtained a promise from a German journal to print Wittgenstein's work; but it was only when Russell recovered and returned to Britain that arrangements were made for a book publisher to bring it out in English and German.

On the whole, Wittgenstein lived up to expectations as a dedicated and gifted schoolteacher. He was diligent and resourceful, according to the acting headmaster in Trattenbach, where Wittgenstein made many of his own teaching aids together with the children. In his various postings during nearly six years as a teacher, he made, among other things, a model steam engine constructed out of wood, a toy ironworks, a potter's wheel, meticulous skeletons, and conducted several trips to Vienna with the children to visit museums and other sites. He also produced a somewhat haphazard spelling book, which was published, though apparently never used in schools. Innovative in his methods and ambitious for his pupils, Wittgenstein was too diligent for some parents. He kept the children in class too long, and sometimes urged the more promising ones to pursue their studies further than their parents deemed useful. His critics thought he was too strict, and he evidently lacked patience with some pupils, especially girls who giggled.

Some villagers in Trattenbach found him standoffish. Wittgenstein's background was a sensitive subject for him. During teacher training, he had fibbed that he was "only distantly" related to the rich Wittgensteins, and he was most upset when the Trattenbachers found out who he was. Hermine was more sympathetic than Paul about this, but she shared his surprise that Ludwig could have thought that he might pass for one of the common herd. "People will have long taken notice of you," she wrote to him, "for our facial features alone betray a good family, not to mention how we talk and think etc!"[13] The commanding self-assurance that was later noted by his pupils in Cambridge confirms that Wittgenstein did not lose his princely affect when he shed his money and his tie.

After a year in Trattenbach, Wittgenstein wrote to Russell that the locals were awful and that he would probably stay there for just one more year, since he did not even get on with the other teachers.[14] He did, though, enjoy the teaching, as he emphasized to Russell later. In November 1921, Russell informed him that his treatise was at last going to be published. It would be printed in a wide-ranging journal edited by a German chemist and polymath, Wilhelm Ostwald, and then, with an English translation, in a new series of books edited by a Cambridge friend, C. K. Ogden.

Ostwald had won the Nobel Prize for chemistry, but to Wittgenstein he was "an utter charlatan," a term he used loosely and often. Ostwald was a man of many theories, and many enthusiasms, one of which was international languages such as Esperanto. Wittgenstein regarded such artificial languages as "despicable" because they did not develop organically, which may explain some or all of his contempt for Ostwald.[15]

Wittgenstein's treatise appeared in early 1922 as the longest article in what turned out to be the last issue of Ostwald's journal, together with pieces about color, geometry, Kant, plants, the Berlin dialect of German, jurisprudence, and assorted other matters. Ogden, meanwhile, arranged for an English translation, and the dual-language book was published in November. When he first read Wittgenstein's manuscript, Ogden was amazed that experts had such trouble understanding it. He told Russell that nearly all of its main ideas seemed "so reasonable and intelligible," a remark suggesting that he had in fact grasped little of the book. Ogden was no philosopher, but he had a gift for spotting and promoting writers.[16]

The first draft of the English translation was done by Frank Ramsey, a Cambridge prodigy whose work in philosophy, mathematics, and economics still resounds nearly a century after his death at the age of twenty-six. Ramsey was a schoolboy when Ogden first encountered him and was only eighteen when invited to be Wittgenstein's translator. He was also chosen, while still an undergraduate, to review the *Tractatus* in the leading English-language journal of philosophy. As soon as he had taken his final exams, Ramsey made a pilgrimage to see Wittgenstein in his village school in 1923, and again several times in 1924. When Wittgenstein returned to Cambridge in 1929, he stayed with Ramsey for a while, later crediting their final conversations with having helped him to see the "grave mistakes" in the *Tractatus*.[17]

Wittgenstein was teaching in the village of Puchberg when Ramsey first visited him in September 1923. "I am now in another hole," he had written to Russell, "though I have to say, it is no better than the old one. Living with human beings is hard! Only they are not really human, but rather 1/4 animal and 3/4 human." Despite such travails, Wittgenstein taught the Puchberg children "with a passion which left nothing more to be desired," according to one of his colleagues, and he made a lifelong friend of another, the school's music teacher, Rudolf Koder, with whom he played.[18] Wittgenstein had now learned an instrument, the clarinet. He wrote to his brother Paul from Puchberg that he was practicing Brahms's Clarinet Quintet, which had been performed in their home in Brahms's presence when Ludwig was two.

During the fortnight of Ramsey's visit, Wittgenstein discussed the *Tractatus* with him every afternoon: "He seems to enjoy this," Ramsey wrote to Ogden, "though he says that his mind is no longer flexible and he can never write another book."[19] Ramsey described the scene to his mother: "He has one tiny room whitewashed, containing a bed, washstand, small table and one hard chair and that is all there is room for. His evening meal which I shared last night is rather unpleasant coarse bread butter and cocoa. . . . In explaining his philosophy he is excited and makes vigorous gestures but relieves the tension by a charming laugh. . . . He is great. I used to think Moore a great man but beside W!"[20] Ramsey was keen to pick Wittgenstein's brain for his own work, which at the time consisted of "reconstructing mathematics," as he put it. This involved using some of Wittgenstein's ideas to reformulate the thesis that mathematics is part of logic. Ramsey had already written his detailed and incisive review of the *Tractatus*. The review did not touch on the troublesome fact that the book had proclaimed itself to be a sort of nonsense. But in a later essay, Ramsey did not pull his punch. If philosophy is nonsense, he wrote, "we must then take seriously that it is nonsense, and not pretend, as Wittgenstein does, that it is important nonsense!"[21]

When he returned to England, Ramsey wrote to Wittgenstein that his own work was not going well because he was distracted by a passion for a married woman, and was so upset that he "nearly resorted to psychoanalysis." In the spring of 1924, Ramsey moved to Vienna for six months and did resort to it. On his third day in Vienna, he called on Gretl, whose eldest son, Thomas, a mathematics undergraduate at Cambridge, he had recently got to know. Ramsey was awed by the baroque palace with "innumerable reception rooms" that served as Gretl's town house. In his letters home, he described her as highly intelligent, knowledgeable about mathematics, "a little exhaustingly intense," and "rather a *grande dame*."[22] Ramsey became a regular guest at Gretl's salons. He went to concerts and the opera, worked on the philosophy of mathematics, and spent an hour each day with his analyst, who was one of Freud's first pupils. Ramsey sometimes found it boring to spend so much time talking about himself, and he was somewhat irritated when the analyst, to whom he had lent a copy of the *Tractatus*, commented that its author clearly suffered from a compulsion neurosis. But after six months, Ramsey concluded that his therapy had worked and might even help him with the philosophy of mathematics. The analyst later commented to a friend of Ramsey's that there had not in fact been much wrong with him.

One of the people whom Ramsey met at Gretl's was Moritz Schlick, the occupant of the chair at Vienna University that had been held by Boltzmann (see chapter 3). Schlick studied physics under Max Planck, the founder of quantum mechanics, and published one of the first philosophical commentaries on the work of Einstein, with whom he became friends. He did not share the contempt for philosophy that Boltzmann had sometimes expressed. That was an outdated attitude, according to Schlick: it was a reaction to the bad old days when scientists "had to defend themselves against the pretensions of philosophers" such as Hegel. The best sort of contemporary philosophy, Schlick argued, worked with the sciences, not against them. Philosophy is "not a separate science to be placed alongside of or above the individual disciplines," he had written in 1918.[23] The task of philosophy was to clarify and interpret, just as Wittgenstein later wrote in his *Tractatus:*

> 4.112 Philosophy aims at the logical clarification of thoughts.

> Philosophy is not a body of doctrine but an activity.
>
> A philosophical work consists essentially of elucidations.
>
> Philosophy does not result in "philosophical propositions," but rather in the clarification of propositions.

Schlick became seriously interested in the *Tractatus* at around the time of his encounter with Ramsey, and quite possibly because of it. "The more one studies [Wittgenstein's] treatise, the more one is impressed by it," he told a philosopher friend after meeting Ramsey. In December 1924, Schlick wrote to Wittgenstein and asked if he could call on him: "There are a number of people here—I am one myself—who are convinced of the importance and correctness of your fundamental ideas." Wittgenstein replied that a visit from Schlick would give him great pleasure, though they did not in fact meet until several years later. When their paths at last crossed in 1927, Schlick effused to Einstein that his talks with Wittgenstein were "among the most powerful intellectual experiences of my life" and that the *Tractatus* was "the deepest and truest work of the new philosophy."[24]

Ramsey went to see Wittgenstein several times during his six months in Austria in 1924, but did not find him to be good value. He wrote to his mother that "it isn't really any good talking to him about work, he won't listen. If you suggest a question he won't listen to your answer but starts thinking of one for himself." Ramsey had not lost his admiration for Wittgenstein's intellect. But, unlike Schlick, he was not content to be a mere disciple: there were philosophical matters to be sorted out, and Wittgenstein could be annoyingly self-absorbed. Keynes and Ramsey were nonetheless keen to lure him back to England, at least for a visit, though Ramsey thought there was little hope of getting him to budge from his present "ridiculous waste of . . . energy and brain" as a schoolteacher.[25] Wittgenstein's psychological problem, Ramsey believed, was somehow the result of his strict upbringing.

Keynes offered to do anything in his power to enable him to do further work, but Wittgenstein responded that "the spring has run dry."[26] This does not quite square with what Ramsey found when he visited him. Wittgenstein had gushed with philosophical thoughts; he just wouldn't listen to Ramsey's. And he had not rebuffed Schlick's overtures. Wittgenstein's feelings about philosophy must have been mixed, as they often were again in later life.

He did, however, decide to spend some of the next year's summer holiday in England, visiting friends in Manchester and Cambridge, and staying for six days as Keynes's guest in Sussex in August 1925. Wittgenstein was not at ease at Keynes's house party, perhaps because it was too social an occasion. Some of Keynes's relatives were there, and Virginia Woolf and her husband, and the Russian ballerina Lydia Lopokova, whom Keynes had just married. Keynes had described Wittgenstein to Lydia as "the mad philosopher genius," and Wittgenstein seems to have behaved with a fierce unconventionality on this occasion. "What a beautiful tree," Lydia remarked to him, whereupon he demanded to know what she meant, and she burst into tears. Ramsey was at the party, too, and he also had an altercation with Wittgenstein, who became annoyed with him. They then had only the coolest of dealings until Wittgenstein moved back to Cambridge four years later, when the spat was forgotten. The trouble seems to have been about Freud. Ramsey confessed to his fiancée, Lettice Baker, that he had got rather heated "because W said that Freud was morally deficient though very clever." Wittgenstein often expressed reservations about Freud. He later wrote in a diary that there was a great deal in what Freud had to say, but "as far as his character is concerned is probably a swine or something similar."[27] Gretl had had similar thoughts:

there was an ethical dimension missing from psychoanalysis, she had thought in her youth, though she later consulted and befriended Freud, and helped him to leave Nazi Vienna.

When Wittgenstein returned from this awkward visit to England, he wrote to Keynes that he would stay in his school job for as long as it inflicted the sort of pain that did his character some good—provided that the "people here don't turn me out." He had been teaching for the past year in the village of Otterthal, where he was remembered as "very strict, but kind-hearted."[28] Postcards to two other friends suggest he had an inkling that his schoolmastering days would not last much longer. If he did give up teaching, he told Keynes, he would probably look for a job in England because he was certain he would not find anything suitable in Austria.

Six months later, Wittgenstein suddenly left his school, but did stay in Austria. In April 1926, just when he turned thirty-seven, he became once more an assistant gardener at a religious institution, this time in a cloister of Hospitallers in Hütteldorf, on the outskirts of Vienna. He had not exactly been turned out by the people of Otterthal, but he did leave under a cloud. A sickly boy collapsed in class after Wittgenstein had hit him, and Wittgenstein resigned, although the official to whom he submitted his resignation urged him not to leave. There was some sort of inquiry, which went on for several months while he was in Hüttledorf and which required him to submit to an examination of his mental competence. "I am curious to know what the psychiatrist will have to say," Wittgenstein wrote to his friend Koder. "I'm sickened by the inquiry and the whole swinish business."[29] It is not clear what the upshot of the inquiry was. Some accounts suggest that he later confessed to having lied about his treatment of the boy. A decade after the incident, when Wittgenstein felt a need to divulge various sins to his closest friends and family, the Otterthal episode featured in his abject confessions, and he went back to the village to apologize to some of his former pupils.

Back in Vienna, Wittgenstein did not spend all of his time cloistered in the Hütteldorf gardens; he began to see a lot of his sister Gretl. This did both of them good, she wrote to her son Thomas in May. The following month, she had even better news to impart: Ludwig was going to help with the design of her new house. For the next two years, Wittgenstein rewardingly exhausted himself as a dilettante architect, with striking results. "You think philosophy is difficult, but I can tell you it is nothing to the difficulty of being a good architect," he later remarked to a Cambridge pupil. He told another that he became so engrossed in interior design that one day when he was ill with a fever, he "thought he was a chair."[30] He had dabbled in design before, offering meticulous commentary on a planned nursery for his Manchester friend Eccles, and teaching the children in Puchberg how to make tables and chairs.

The initial architect for Gretl's house was Wittgenstein's friend Paul Engelmann, who had done work for several members of the family. Gretl owned a country estate, the Villa Toscana, which was built for the family of a grand duke of Tuscany, and rented apartments in Vienna's Palais Schönborn-Batthyány—the baroque place that had awed Ramsey—but now wanted to build her own modernist house in Vienna. In November 1925 she invited Engelmann to draw up plans, and Wittgenstein became very interested in the project while he was still teaching in Otterthal. His comments on the first sketches led Engelmann to offer him a partnership, and Wittgenstein gave up gardening and began his new career in earnest in late August 1926. A third architect was also involved, since Engelmann had no experience in construction, but Wittgenstein soon became in effect the senior partner. According to Engelmann: "He was the actual architect. . . . I regard the result as his achievement, not mine."[31]

Wittgenstein shared his family's fastidious connoisseurship in matters of design, which in his case was marked by a preference for simplicity. "He is *very* fussy," Russell told Morrell when Wittgenstein was fitting out his first college rooms in 1912. "He dislikes all ornamentation that is not part of the construction, and can never find anything simple enough." Wittgenstein once took Pinsent shopping for furniture, which was very amusing, Pinsent recorded in his diary: "We led the shopman a frightful dance, Wittgenstein ejaculating 'No—Beastly!' to 90% of what he showed us!" Since nothing pleased him, Wittgenstein had his furniture made to order. After he left Cambridge for Norway in 1913, Russell bought it from him, and Russell's children later came to know of Wittgenstein as "the giver of beautiful things." Wittgenstein also took Pinsent to a scientific-equipment shop in East London to buy porcelain mugs. He always used chemical beakers, Pinsent recorded, "because ordinary crockery is too ugly for him."[32]

Engelmann was a former pupil of Adolf Loos, whose attacks on superfluous ornamentation were praised in Kraus's *Die Fackel* when Gretl and Ludwig were eager readers of it. "The evolution of culture," Loos declared in a partly jokey lecture "Ornament and Crime," is "synonymous with the removal of ornamentation from objects of everyday use." Wittgenstein had met Loos in Vienna before the war, and they remained friends, despite one scornful Wittgensteinian outburst to Engelmann about the "bogus intellectualism" of a pamphlet Loos had written.[33] Wittgenstein and Gretl visited Loos during the construction of the house, but it is not known whether Loos ever saw it. The stark, unadorned cubic volumes of its exterior and some split levels inside are similar to some of his work, but opinion is divided on the question of how Loosian the house is.

Visitors to the completed house remarked on its "stunning

House designed by Ludwig Wittgenstein for his sister Gretl, circa 1928.
(© Françoise and Pierre Stonborough / Wittgenstein Initiative)

and liberating" spaces as well as its "airy, harmonious and perfect" feel. In her family memoir, Hermine described some of the work that went into producing such effects: "Ludwig designed every window and door, every window-lock and radiator, with as much care and attention to detail as if they were precision instruments, and on a most elegant scale. . . . I can still hear the locksmith asking him, in connection with a keyhole, 'Tell me, Herr Ingenieur, does a millimetre here or there really matter so much to you?' Even before he had finished speaking, Ludwig replied with such a loud, forceful 'Yes!' that the man almost jumped with fright."[34] She also singled out the unusually high glass doors, which were so nearly impossible to construct that a contractor was reduced to sobbing. And she extolled a soothing pair of L-shaped radiators: "Just the symmetry of the two black objects in the light room gives one a feeling of well-being! . . . It became clear that the kind of thing Ludwig had in mind could not be cast anywhere in Austria. . . . Whole batches of pipe sections had to be rejected as unusable, others had to be machined to an accuracy of within half a millimetre. . . . Under Ludwig's direction, experiments often went on into the night, until finally everything was just as it should be. In fact a whole year passed between the design of these radiators, seemingly so simple, and their delivery."[35]

Wittgenstein's work on the house let him indulge in the mechanical tinkering that he had so enjoyed as a boy. He designed its internal telephone system and a network of servants' bells. Conceived on a grand scale, the house and its garden filled a city block, and was planned to include seven bedrooms for servants as well as rooms for a dressmaker and a governess. It was "such a princely gesture that you can't do anything but live in it like a prince," Hermine observed.[36]

Wittgenstein spent two years working on Gretl's house until it was finished in the autumn of 1928, during which time he had two consequential encounters. One was with Marguerite Respinger, an unintellectual woman of twenty-two whom Gretl's son Thomas had befriended in Cambridge. Gretl took "little Marguerite" under her wing and into her homes, where she met Wittgenstein while he was recuperating at his sister's after suffering an injury at the building site. He often unwound with Marguerite at the cinema after a day's work, and although he was never quite sure what he wanted from her, he fell in love with her. Their confused romance bloomed and wilted from 1929 to 1933, while Wittgenstein was in Cambridge during academic terms and in Austria for most of the holidays.

It was also while he was working on the house that Wittgenstein finally met Schlick and gingerly began to talk about philosophy again. Gretl invited Schlick for lunch in February 1927. She had told him that her brother was too focused on his architecture to have discussions with a group of people, which is what Schlick had suggested, but that he was happy to talk to just Schlick. After their lunch, Wittgenstein relented and agreed to several meetings with Schlick and some of his colleagues. Schlick's group came to be known as the Vienna Circle, and their stance was later dubbed "logical positivism." Positivism in philosophy means optimism about the scope and benefits of science, together with a suspicion of any purported knowledge that is not rooted in sensory experience. The Viennese version of positivism was "logical" because it championed the new logic of Frege and Russell as a tool that could make philosophy more scientific.

The Vienna Circle published a manifesto in 1929, "The Scientific Conception of the World," which rallied troops for an attack on "the metaphysical and theological debris of millennia." It singled out the ideas of Russell and Wittgenstein as especially useful for exposing "the logical origins of metaphysical aberration." The circle hoped to divide and conquer the problems of philosophy by sorting them into two groups. Some problems would be reshaped so that they could be handled by scientific methods, just as Russell had urged, and the rest would be exposed as mere "pseudo-problems."[37]

According to Schlick, a turning point had been reached in philosophy, thanks above all to Wittgenstein's *Tractatus*. It had revealed that the supposedly unanswerable questions of traditional philosophy were, as Schlick put it, "not genuine questions, but meaningless concatenations of words."[38] And one ought to observe silence about such unspeakable things, just as the *Tractatus* had declared.

Yet there was a large difference between Wittgenstein's outlook and that of the Vienna Circle. As Engelmann put it in his memoir: "Positivism holds—and this is its essence—that what we can speak about is all that matters in life. *Whereas Wittgenstein passionately believes that all that really matters in human life is precisely what, in his view, we must be silent about.*"[39] There are "things that cannot be put into words," Wittgenstein had written in the *Tractatus*. "They *make themselves manifest.* They are what is mystical." But no such things made themselves manifest to the positivists. They gratefully echoed Wittgenstein's attack on meaningless philosophizing: "Most of the propositions and questions to be found in philosophical works are not false but nonsensical," he had declared in the *Tractatus*.[40] But they declined his mysticism.

When Schlick introduced Wittgenstein to some of his group in the summer of 1927, he warned them to tread carefully because the great man was "very sensitive and easily disturbed by a direct question." According to one of them, Herbert Feigl, Wittgenstein was reluctant to discuss philosophical matters, and on one occasion read some poetry by Tagore to them instead. Wittgenstein told them, as he told Keynes, that he had said everything he had to say in the *Tractatus*. Yet on the occasions when they could get him to discuss the book, Feigl reported, Wittgenstein "couldn't reconstruct any more just what he meant when writing it." Despite his stated unwillingness to talk about philosophy, he did in fact do so enough for the group to witness "his most impressive and highly intuitive approach to various philosophical problems."[41] One thing they discussed at their meetings, which were usually at Schlick's home or in a café, was a recently published paper by Ramsey on the foundations of mathematics.

Another member of the group, Rudolf Carnap, heard enough of Wittgenstein's philosophizing to reach a conclusion about his inner struggles and their bearing on his views:

> When Schlick . . . made a critical remark about a metaphysical statement by a classical philosopher (I think it was Schopenhauer), Wittgenstein surprisingly turned against Schlick and defended the philosopher and his work.
>
> These and similar occurrences in our conversations showed that there was a strong inner conflict in Wittgenstein between his emotional life and his intellectual thinking. His intellect . . . had recognized that many statements in the field of religion and metaphysics did not, strictly speaking, say anything. In his characteristic absolute honesty with himself, he did not try to shut his eyes to this insight. But this result was extremely painful for him emotionally, as if he were compelled to admit a weakness in a beloved person. Schlick, and I, by contrast, had no love for metaphysics or metaphysical theology, and therefore could abandon them without inner conflict or regret.[42]

Like Russell fifteen years earlier, both Carnap and Feigl were struck by what they took to be Wittgenstein's artistic temperament. Feigl thought that if the circumstances of his life had been different, "the genius of Wittgenstein might well have expressed itself in art or music." Wittgenstein himself sometimes wished that it had: "I often think that the highest I wish to achieve would be to compose a melody," he wrote in his diary in 1930.[43]

Carnap felt that one might almost compare him to a prophet as well as to an artist because of the way his revelations came to him: "When finally, sometimes after a prolonged arduous effort, his answer came forth, his statement stood before us like a newly created piece of art or a divine revelation. Not that he asserted his views dogmatically . . . he often expressed the feeling that his statements were inadequate. But the impression he made on us was as if insight came to him as through a divine inspiration, so that we could not help feeling that any sober rational comment or analysis of it would be a profanation."[44]

In March 1928, with some difficulty, members of the circle persuaded Wittgenstein to attend a lecture, "Mathematics, Science, and Language," by a Dutch mathematician, L. E. J. Brouwer. Brouwer had developed a novel philosophy of mathematics, known as intuitionism, that emphasizes the role of human invention in mathematics. Wittgenstein later described intuitionism as "all bosh," but he appeared to be interested by the lecture. Immediately after it, he talked volubly about philosophy at great length in a café. Looking back four decades later, Feigl reckoned that this had been "a great event," because it seemed to mark Wittgenstein's return to philosophy.[45]

Nothing happened immediately. Gretl's house was not finished for another six months or so, but soon after his work as an architect was over, Wittgenstein wrote to Keynes that he wanted to come to Cambridge for a visit, and as soon as he arrived, he announced that he planned to stay. Russell was no longer at Cambridge, and their relationship seems to have cooled slightly, at least on Wittgenstein's side. But the place still had Keynes, Ramsey, and Moore—Wittgenstein's rows with the latter two were forgotten when he returned. One pupil had the impression that Wittgenstein was driven to come back by a desire to correct his former views; another was told that it was because "I felt at that time that I had thought more, and more successfully, about certain problems than others had done."[46] Moore speculated that it was in order to have frequent talks with Ramsey. Wittgenstein seems to have felt for quite a while that he had unfinished business at Cambridge. While he was still a schoolteacher, he had asked Ramsey to find out what he would have to do in order to complete his Cambridge degree.

Work on architecture is "work on oneself," as is work on philosophy, Wittgenstein reflected in a notebook. He seems to have regarded everything he did as work on himself. He was proud of what he had achieved with Gretl's house, and sent some photographs of it to Keynes, hoping he would not be "too much disgusted by its simplicity." Wittgenstein was less proud of the work he had done on himself as a schoolteacher. According to Marguerite Respinger, he was "very unsatisfied and felt guilty" about that time—guilty, presumably, because of the boy he had struck.[47]

Yet Wittgenstein's days in village classrooms had, as Engelmann noticed, changed the way he did philosophy. In Wittgenstein's later work, he prodded his readers along by posing questions that they were supposed to answer for themselves, just as his young pupils in Trattenbach, Puchberg, and Otterthal would have been expected to do. Hermine observed these methods when he came to Vienna and gave some lessons to the boys in an occupational school with which she was involved: "He did not simply lecture, but tried to lead the boys to the correct solution by means of questions." This is also how he proceeded in his posthumously published *Philosophical Investigations.* The book contains 784 questions, according to one analysis, of which nearly 90 percent are left unanswered, and most of the rest receive an answer that is presented as wrong.[48] His lectures in the 1930s and 1940s proceeded in a similar way.

Wittgenstein's years with children appear to have affected not only his manner of exposition but also the substance of his thought. There is not a single mention in the *Tractatus* or in his early notebooks, dictations, or letters about how one learns or teaches anything. But discussions of teaching and learning are ubiquitous in his later writings and are to be found again and again in accounts of his lectures. After he returned to philosophy in 1929, Wittgenstein frequently addressed philosophical questions by examining how one would learn or teach the concepts involved in them. "One thing we [his Cambridge classes] always do when discussing a word," he reflected to his pupils in 1938, "is to ask how we were taught it."[49]

Although Keynes was eager for Wittgenstein to return to Cambridge, he knew how exhausting it was to be with him. "Am I strong enough?" he wrote to Lydia when Wittgenstein suggested coming for a fortnight. The visit was planned for early December 1928, but postponed because of a cold. "Pray for me!" Keynes wrote on the eve of Wittgenstein's appearance in January 1929.

"Well, God has arrived," he drily wrote to Lydia the next day. "I met him on the 5.15 train. He has a plan to stay in Cambridge permanently."[50]

6

The Stream of Life

WORDS HAVE MEANING "only in the stream of life," wrote Wittgenstein near the end of his. This saying might almost serve as a slogan for the philosophy he developed after his return to Cambridge in 1929. In his early work, he had focused on propositions and their relations to one another and to the world. Later, he stood back to survey language in a broader landscape, regarding it as "part of an activity, or of a form of life."[1] He still held that philosophical problems arise only because "the logic of our language is misunderstood," as he had put it in the *Tractatus.* But he came to think that grasping this logic required one to be a sort of anthropologist. One had to observe language in its habitat, examining how its tools are normally acquired and wielded.

In *Philosophical Investigations,* the most polished product of his later thinking, Wittgenstein put it like this:

> When philosophers use a word—"knowledge," "being," "object," "I," "proposition/sentence," "name"—and try to grasp the *essence* of the thing, one must always ask oneself: is the word ever actually used in this way in the language in which it is at home?—
>
> What *we* do is to bring words back from their metaphysical to their everyday use.[2]

Philosophical problems arise, he wrote, "when *language goes on holiday.*" During such jaunts, words float away from their moorings, and needless perplexity ensues—or so Wittgenstein thought. One example of what he seems to have had in mind is the raising of philosophical doubts about everyday things. Can we, for instance, be certain that anything physical exists? Russell addressed such questions in his little 1912 book, *The Problems of Philosophy*, as did many other philosophers before and after him. In his final writings, Wittgenstein aimed to undermine this sort of skepticism rather than to answer it directly. He suggested that it is a misunderstanding of the nature of inquiry to believe that we can challenge everything: "The *questions* that we raise and our *doubts* depend on the fact that some propositions are exempt from doubt. . . . My *life* consists in my being content to accept many things."[3]

Wittgenstein credited Ramsey, and especially another Cambridge friend, Piero Sraffa, with helping him to change his point of view. Sraffa was an Italian economist with whom he had over two hundred meetings between 1929 and 1946. Although their talks seem mainly not to have focused on philosophy, Wittgenstein told a pupil that it was from Sraffa that he learned to see philosophical problems in an "anthropological" way. Even mathematics was "after all an anthropological phenomenon," Wittgenstein came to think. Sraffa once made a Neapolitan gesture and presented it as a challenge to Wittgenstein's analysis of propositions. There are conflicting accounts of what exactly was said, but Wittgenstein singled out the episode as providing something of a revelation about the nature of meaning. Sraffa was nonplussed to be told after Wittgenstein's death that he had made such an impact on the great philosopher. It seemed to him that the points he had put to Wittgenstein were "rather obvious."[4]

Wittgenstein's talks with Ramsey spanned only one year because Ramsey died after a brief illness in January 1930. But the two made much of what time they had. When he first arrived back in Cambridge, Wittgenstein lived with Ramsey and his wife, Lettice, for a while, and thereafter returned regularly to their house for discussions in Ramsey's study, and for musical evenings and dinners. According to Keynes, Lettice exerted a calming influence that made Wittgenstein "more 'normal' in every way than I have ever known him." In February 1929, his second month back at Cambridge, Wittgenstein recorded that he was having "very enjoyable discussions with Ramsey about logic etc. They are rather like a vigorous sport and I believe are conducted in a good spirit. There is something erotic and chivalrous about them. They give me a sort of intellectual courage."[5]

Ramsey, in turn, enthused in a letter to Schlick about how stimulating it was to talk with Wittgenstein, and he attested to Trinity College that Wittgenstein was a "philosophic genius of a different order from anyone else I know. This is partly owing to his great gift for seeing what is essential in a problem and partly to his overwhelming intellectual vigour." The vigor could be wearying, though, as Ramsey confided to a friend. Wittgenstein was "very nice, but rather dogmatic and inclined to repeat explanations of simple things. Because if you doubt the truth of what he says he always thinks you can't have understood it." Wittgenstein sometimes worked himself up into quite a state during these sporting encounters in Ramsey's study; "I am so horrible," Lettice once overheard him say after a protracted silence from within.[6]

Ramsey, who turned twenty-six in February, was officially

the supervisor of Wittgenstein's research. His forty-one-year-old pupil was granted a doctorate in June after a viva voce examination at which he was questioned on the *Tractatus* by Russell and Moore. Russell was at the time running a progressive school in Sussex with his second wife, Dora, and visited Cambridge for the event, which was a mere formality. Although Wittgenstein always professed disdain for the academic life and its trappings, the doctorate seems to have mattered to him, since Ramsey was obliged to rebut some almost paranoid concerns about it. "But, Ludwig," he wrote, "it really isn't true that I didn't care twopence whether you got your degree."[7] Keynes, too, had to defend himself against Wittgenstein's fanciful sensitivities. Of course he never believed that Wittgenstein cultivated their friendship to get money out of him, Keynes protested in the spring of 1929. He called Wittgenstein a maniac for thinking so. The soothing influence of Lettice Ramsey seems to have been only temporary.

Some of Ramsey's last writings hint at what it was that may have helped to point Wittgenstein in new directions. "In the process of clarifying our thought," Ramsey argued in one essay, "we come to terms and sentences which we cannot elucidate in the obvious manner by defining their meaning . . . but we can explain the way in which they are used." This became a theme of Wittgenstein's later work. The biggest mistake made by philosophers, he told some pupils in 1938, "is that when language is looked at, what is looked at is a form of words and not the use made of the form of words."[8] Ramsey was keen on the "pragmatism" of the American philosopher C. S. Peirce, which sought to relate the truth of a belief to the usefulness of holding it. This interest in pragmatism seems to have rubbed off on Wittgenstein for a while. But he always developed his own idiosyncratic take on the influences he absorbed. One can only guess which seeds Ramsey planted and how they began to grow.

* * *

Some of Wittgenstein's work in his first few years back at Cambridge consisted of tinkering with the *Tractatus*. He wrote a paper in which he tackled a problem Ramsey had pressed in his review of the book—that its account of tautologies could not easily cope with the kind of necessity expressed by the proposition that a patch of color cannot be both red and green. But before the time came for Wittgenstein to deliver his paper, which was written for an academic conference, he came to think that it was no good, and decided to talk instead about generality and infinity in mathematics. That will be much more fun, he wrote to Russell, urging him to attend the event. Infinity was one of many topics Wittgenstein was exploring in his notebooks at the time. His views were in flux and did not gel for a few years.

In November 1929, Wittgenstein gave a public talk in which he still sounded very "Tractatussy," as one pupil put it. It was an address to the Heretics Society, a distinguished Cambridge club, in which he repeated his old idea that ethical matters cannot be captured in words. To illustrate what he meant by "absolute or ethical value," Wittgenstein mentioned two experiences. The first was the experience of marveling at the existence of the world—that is, of feeling it to be extraordinary that there should be anything at all. The second was "the experience of feeling *absolutely* safe," like the surpassing sense of security that had moved him while watching a Viennese comedy.[9]

One might wonder what either of these feelings has to do with ethics. Wittgenstein evidently had a broad conception of the topic. He ended his presentation with a personal statement: "My whole tendency and I believe the tendency of all men who ever tried to write or talk ethics or religion was to run against the boundaries of language. This running against the walls of our cage is perfectly, absolutely, hopeless.—Ethics, so far as it springs from the desire to say something about the ultimate meaning of life, the absolute good . . . can be no science. What it says does not add to our knowledge in any sense. But it is a document of a tendency in the human mind which I personally cannot help respecting deeply and I would not for my life ridicule it."[10] It was "a magnificent speech . . . though it was wasted on the Heretics, who cannot appreciate religious feeling," noted one student. Another wrote in her diary that Wittgenstein was "a passionate little Austrian, poor & undernourished looking, but with a noble and fine face that lights up & burns with emotion & intellect."[11]

Back in Vienna for the Christmas holidays, Wittgenstein spoke to Schlick and a member of his circle, Friedrich Waismann, about the talk he had just given. It is important, Wittgenstein told them, "to put an end to all the claptrap about ethics . . . whether values exist, whether the good is definable. In ethics we are always making the attempt to say something that cannot be said."[12] Wittgenstein apparently decided to put an end to his public talks as well. He gave no more lectures to general audiences after 1929, nor did he attend any more academic conferences.

Wittgenstein returned to Vienna for most of the Cambridge vacations in the 1930s, and never missed a family Christmas until the German annexation of Austria in 1938. He often met Schlick and Waismann on these visits, until Schlick's death in 1936, and Waismann usually took notes of their discussions. In the first few of these meetings, Wittgenstein made comments about verification that were seized upon by members of the Vienna Circle. The gist of his remarks became one of the best-known tenets of logical positivism: "In order to determine the sense of a proposition," he told Schlick and Waismann in December 1929, "I should have to know a very specific procedure for when to count the proposition as verified." And if the sense of a proposition cannot be verified completely, he said, then it "signifies nothing whatsoever." Wittgenstein made similar remarks in some Cambridge lectures in 1931–32: "The meaning of a proposition is the mode of its verification. . . . Ethical and aesthetic judgements are not propositions because they cannot be verified." Like some other positivists, Carnap based his dismissal of metaphysics on what he called "Wittgenstein's principle of verifiability," which Carnap defined as the principle that "the meaning of a sentence is given by the conditions of its verification and . . . a sentence is meaningful if and only if it is in principle verifiable."[13]

The Vienna Circle's emphasis on verification had a notable precursor in the writings of one of its ancestors, Ernst Mach, who held the university chair later occupied by Boltzmann and Schlick. "Where neither confirmation nor refutation is possible, science is not concerned," Mach had declared in 1883. Wittgenstein's originality was sometimes overestimated by members of the circle, especially Schlick, but it does seem to have been Wittgenstein who prompted them to revive Mach's focus on verification. When Wittgenstein once jocularly remarked, "Hell, Blazes, I founded the Logical Positivists," this was not just vanity, though it was an exaggeration.[14]

Wittgenstein himself soon came to believe that verification was less important than he had thought. He could be as restless in his philosophical opinions as he was in other respects. To ask how an assertion could be verified was "just one way among others of getting clear about the use of a word or sentence," he said in the late 1930s.[15] An equally useful way, he added, is to ask how a word is learned or taught. He came to employ "logical positivist" as a term of abuse, using it rather liberally to include various Oxford and Cambridge thinkers who had incurred his displeasure.

During Wittgenstein's visits to Vienna, there was time for a sort of love as well as for philosophy. He kissed the young Marguerite Respinger "a lot for three hours and it was very nice," he wrote in his diary during the Easter vacation of 1930. He wrote to her often when he was in Cambridge, sometimes almost daily, and confided to Lettice Ramsey that he was in love—"very much in love," according to his diary. But Marguerite could not determine what kind of love it was. She revealed to Gretl in autumn 1929 that Wittgenstein had said, "I have a feeling for you, like for a sister with whom one is a little in love" and had suggested that she become his housekeeper.[16]

The situation with Marguerite was tortuous, Wittgenstein felt in 1931, and he dreaded losing her. Marriage was sometimes spoken of, though he would contemplate only a chaste union. In early 1932, Gretl intervened. Adept at managing the personal lives of her two younger brothers, she firmly spelled out to Ludwig that Marguerite needed a conventional marriage. He would not, Gretl told him, be able to have the sort of relationship with her that he wanted until after "she is sexually . . . bound to another man."[17]

Wittgenstein was more or less aware of this already. "M. needs me as a corrective but not as her sole proprietor," he had recorded in his diary. He saw himself as Marguerite's guide and instructor: she was to give up her ambition to be an artist because she did not have enough talent. Wittgenstein was most gratified when she began charitable work in a home for infants, but she was not happy there, and left. He then took her to Skjolden for a summer holiday in 1931, a trip that he described to a pupil as "looking for a job for my lady friend."[18] She was deposited at lodgings in the town with a copy of the Bible and told to reflect on her situation, while he stayed in his former house. Wittgenstein subsequently appointed himself as a corrective to several Cambridge pupils and younger friends, usually suggesting that they pursue menial or at least practical rather than intellectual forms of work. One symptom of his uncertainty about what to do with his life was a penchant for telling other people what to do with theirs.

Wittgenstein's Cambridge teaching career began in earnest on 20 January 1930 with a lecture in which he announced,

"Philosophy is the attempt to be rid of a particular kind of puzzlement." The sort of perplexity he had in mind was "irrelevant to our everyday life," he said, and was generated by "puzzles of *language*." (Moore was there, and listed "What is reality? What is number? Are Space and Time real?" as examples.)[19] For most of the next seventeen years, Wittgenstein sought to dispel puzzlement among Cambridge philosophers and students, with a break of nearly two years, 1936–38, that he spent mostly in Norway trying to write a book, and three years of war work at hospitals in the early 1940s. Although none of his pupils claimed to have been wholly purged of philosophical perplexity, many were enthralled by Wittgenstein's forceful efforts to address philosophical problems in a new way.

Most of his lectures and discussion classes were given to small groups gathered in his bare rooms at the top of a Victorian tower in Trinity, the same eyrie he had occupied for a year in 1912–13. Wooden chairs were brought in for students, but otherwise the room contained only one or two canvas deck chairs, a card table for writing, a safe for his manuscripts, perhaps a vase of flowers, and sometimes a book or two. Next door was his camp bed and a bathtub. In these stark surroundings and at meetings of the university's philosophy society, the Moral Sciences Club, Wittgenstein's Cambridge cult was formed.

When Russell had been due to give some lectures at Harvard in 1914, the young Wittgenstein urged him to "tell them your *thoughts* and not *just* cut and dried results." This became Wittgenstein's own practice: he thought aloud, usually without notes, alternating between fluent, vividly illustrated disquisitions and agonized silences and groans as he struggled to harvest his freshest ideas. Even one pupil who thought that Wittgenstein was wrong about almost everything conceded that his most faltering pronouncement sounded as if "it sprang from a mind of supreme integrity and the most penetrating insight." Some of Wittgenstein's followers found themselves aping the mannerisms of their charismatic and sometimes frightening master. When an Oxford philosopher, Isaiah Berlin, visited the Moral Sciences Club in 1940, he recounted that the "small and handsome" Wittgenstein was "surrounded with acolytes in tweed jackets and white shirts identical to his own."[20] Berlin, who enjoyed gossip, perhaps embroidered his account, but several pupils acknowledged that they had picked up Wittgenstein's distinctive gestures and speech. The same was said of Waismann in Vienna.

Wittgenstein appeared nervous in his first Cambridge lecture, recording later that it went only "so, so." He was grieving for Ramsey, who had died the previous day in a London hospital, where Wittgenstein had just visited him. He ought not to have died, Wittgenstein told several people, including Ramsey's father, in a letter that blamed him for his son's death because he had, in Wittgenstein's opinion, mishandled his medical treatment. Three months later, Wittgenstein indulged in some further awkward truth-telling. Although he and Ramsey had been able to communicate on some matters, Wittgenstein wrote in his diary, Ramsey's "incapacity for genuine enthusiasm or genuine reverence, which is the same, finally repulsed me more & more." Ramsey had "an ugly mind," Wittgenstein wrote. But he did not have an "ugly soul," because he "truly relished music & with understanding. And one could see by looking at him what effect it had on him."[21]

When Russell reviewed a posthumous collection of Ramsey's papers, he called his achievement amazing but ended with a note of reservation: "His thought was conservative in the sense that he wished to introduce only such changes as were necessary to preserve the substance of the old against revolution." Ramsey may sometimes have been too practical-minded, Russell suggested, and was perhaps not always profound. Wittgenstein echoed this idea: "Ramsey was a bourgeois thinker. I.e. he thought with the aim of clearing up the affairs of some particular community." For Wittgenstein, this meant that Ramsey was not interested in "real philosophical reflection."[22]

Wittgenstein felt estranged not only from Ramsey's way of thinking but from the modern world. He regarded contemporary culture "without sympathy, without understanding its aims if any," he wrote in 1930, in a draft foreword for a proposed book. The spirit of European and American civilization as it was manifested in "the industry, architecture, music, of present day fascism & socialism" was one that he found "alien & uncongenial." As far as Wittgenstein was concerned, the arts had disappeared, and he did not care whether "the typical western scientist" understood or appreciated his work.

His goal was a type of clarity:

> Our civilisation is characterised by the word progress. . . . Its *activity* is to construct a more and more complicated structure. And even clarity is only a means to this & not an end in itself.
>
> For me on the contrary clarity, transparency, is an end in itself.
>
> I am not interested in erecting a building but in having the foundations of possible buildings transparently before me.
>
> So I am aiming at something different than are the scientists & my thoughts move differently than do theirs.[23]

Wittgenstein once told his friend and former pupil Drury that he had passed a bookshop and seen portraits of Russell, Freud, and Einstein in the window, and then "in a music shop, I saw portraits of Beethoven, Schubert and Chopin. Comparing these portraits I felt intensely the terrible degeneration that had come over the human spirit in the course of only a hundred years." Wittgenstein evidently missed the culture that was preserved and honored in his childhood home. His cultural ideal sometimes seemed to him to have come "from the time of Schumann," he said—that is, from the first half of the nineteenth century.[24]

There was at least one Cambridge friend who made similar complaints about modern ways of thinking. Raffaello Piccoli, a professor of Italian literature with whom Wittgenstein talked very frequently from 1929 to 1931, rued "the mechanisation of the spirit and the tyranny of pseudo-scientific ideas," which he saw as a threat to civilization. Scholars of literature and history were "childishly aping the mechanical and mathematical methods of the sciences," Piccoli said in a lecture in 1929. Technical advances had increased "the mechanical dominance of man over the forces of nature," but "the more nature reveals to him the secrets of its structure . . . the less is man capable of maintaining his spiritual dominance."[25]

Wittgenstein and Piccoli shared an aversion to the amateur philosophizing of physicists such as Sir James Jeans and Sir Arthur Eddington. Jeans's *The Mysterious Universe* (1930) was advertised by its publisher as an "entrancing survey of the riddle of existence." To Wittgenstein, such books were "an abomination" because they pandered to superficiality and were full of "absurd . . . semi-philosophical speculations."[26] Russell, too, attacked Jeans and Eddington for sometimes jumping to religious and philosophical conclusions. But Russell saw nothing wrong with trying to explain science to the public, having himself published an *ABC of Atoms* and an *ABC of Relativity* in the 1920s.

When Wittgenstein remarked that music came to a full stop with Brahms, he had added "and even in Brahms I can begin to hear the sound of machinery." The clang of industry was an ominous noise, albeit one that Wittgenstein was, as an engineer, fond of in small doses. On several occasions in the 1940s, he suggested that what may in some respects seem like progress might also be a step backward, and he cited the example of the iron industry, which scarred valleys with "slagheaps and old machinery." It was not absurd, he wrote, to think that the age of science and technology might be "the beginning of the end for humanity."[27] He was thus questioning his father's estimation of the value of mechanization and industry, and decrying the thing that had elevated the Wittgenstein family into a position from which it looked down on others.

After he had been lecturing in Cambridge for three years, reports of Wittgenstein's new ideas began to seep out, which did not please him. In May 1933, he wrote a letter to the editor of *Mind*, the leading English-language philosophy journal, repudiating an account of his views that had been published by Richard Braithwaite, a young Cambridge philosopher. Wittgenstein wrote that he was struggling to present his work in a coherent form, which is why he had not himself published any of it, and why he could not say any more about it in a letter. Braithwaite reasonably responded that the extent to which he had misrepresented Wittgenstein "cannot be judged until the appearance of the book which we are all eagerly awaiting."[28]

No such book appeared until after Wittgenstein's death. In 1933, he produced a typescript based on thousands of pages of remarks that he had written over the past four years, but he kept it to himself. At the end of the year, however, he began to dictate accounts of his ideas to his students. One such dictation, which came to be known as the *Blue Book*, is almost a conventional piece of philosophical writing, consisting of continuous prose rather than Wittgenstein's usual choppy stream of remarks, though it does jump to and fro between topics, which was, as Wittgenstein later confessed, the only way of thinking that was natural to him.

He was sufficiently satisfied with his *Blue Book* to give copies of it to Russell and Sraffa. But he warned that it would be hard to understand for someone who had not been at his lectures. Wittgenstein frequently worried about being misunderstood, misrepresented, or plagiarized. In 1932, he had shocked Carnap by unjustly accusing him of stealing his ideas, which would (he told Carnap) make Wittgenstein himself look like a plagiarist if he ever published them. His fits of umbrage at supposed thefts of his thoughts continued until the last weeks of his life. Paul Wittgenstein also had a fiercely possessive attitude to intellectual property, which in his case concerned the musical works he had commissioned. "You don't build a house just so that someone else can live in it," he informed another one-armed pianist.[29] Paul did everything he could to prevent others from performing the music that had been written for him, even pieces that he disliked and never played. When he did perform one of his commissions, he gathered up scores after concerts so that they would not fall into the wrong hands.

The *Blue Book* was shown only to a trusted few, though pirated copies made their way to Oxford, where they helped to shape a movement that is sometimes called ordinary language philosophy. Wittgenstein was occasionally right to suspect unacknowledged borrowing. One young leader of the Oxford movement, J. L. Austin, was less than forthcoming about his debt to the man he referred to as "poor old Witters."[30]

The language that Wittgenstein explored in his *Blue Book* was mainly the kind used to describe mental activities or states, such as understanding, expecting, or meaning something, or experiencing a sensation of pain. His goal was to show that these things are, in a way, less mental than they seem: "I have been trying in all this to remove the temptation to think that there '*must* be' what is called a mental process of thinking, hoping, wishing, believing, etc., independent of the process of expressing a thought, a hope, a wish, etc." He was not denying that we have inner worlds that we can to a certain extent keep private. Rather, he sought to turn the mind inside out: to reveal how our mental lives are generally played out on a public stage, not confined to private performances in an inner theater. Consider the experience of toothache. A toothache may be mine, in the sense that I have a toothache and you do not. But if I cry out and clutch my jaw, you may know just as well as I do that I am in pain, or so Wittgenstein argued. He wanted to undermine the idea that there are, as he put it, "two kinds of worlds, . . . a mental world and a physical world," the former of which is private and known only to oneself. (Wittgenstein later pursued this theme of inner privacy in some much-discussed passages about a hypothetical "private language.")[31]

Similar ideas were advanced by Oxford philosopher Gilbert Ryle in his book *The Concept of Mind* (1949), which attacked what he called "the dogma of the Ghost in the Machine." According to this dogma, which Ryle blamed on Descartes, "each of us lives the life of a ghostly Robinson Crusoe" inside the machine of our body. Wittgenstein and Ryle were friends in the 1930s and sometimes went on walking holidays together; Ryle later said that he had learned a lot from Wittgenstein. Their styles were very different, though. One Australian philosopher at Oxford remarked that Ryle's views were like Wittgenstein's but "tempered by English common sense and good humour."[32]

According to Wittgenstein, various things tempt us to think of mental states and activities in the wrong way. Many are rooted in the forms of our language, or so he believed—"We are up against trouble caused by our way of expression." Also, we are inclined to ape the generalizing and reductive methods of natural science. We suffer, he said, from a "craving for generality," which can make us leap to wrong conclusions, and cause us to neglect revealing aspects of particular cases.[33] Later, in his *Philosophical Investigations*, Wittgenstein illustrated the temptation to overgeneralize by introducing the idea of "family resemblances" between things that fall under the same general term:

> Consider . . . the activities that we call "games." I mean board-games, card-games, ball-games, athletic games, and so on. What is common to them all?—Don't say: "They *must* have something in common, or they would not be called 'games'"—but *look and see* whether there is anything common to all.—For if you look at them, you won't see something that

> is common to *all*, but similarities, affinities, and a whole series of them at that. . . .
>
> I can think of no better expression to characterize these similarities than "family resemblances"; for the various resemblances between members of a family—build, features, colour of eyes, gait, temperament, and so on and so forth—overlap and criss-cross in the same way.—And I shall say: "games" form a family.[34]

The cure for ills such as our "craving for generality" and philosophical troubles "caused by our way of expression" is a close inspection of the ways we talk in everyday life: "If we scrutinize the usages which we make of such words as 'thinking,' 'meaning,' 'wishing,' etc., going through this process rids us of the temptation to look for a peculiar act of thinking, independent of the act of expressing our thoughts, and stowed away in some peculiar medium. . . . The scrutiny of the grammar of a word [by "grammar" Wittgenstein here meant "proper use"] weakens the position of certain standards of our expression which had prevented us from seeing facts with unbiassed eyes. Our investigation tried to remove this bias, which forces us to think that the facts *must* conform to certain pictures embedded in our language."[35]

Our language is thus both a cause of philosophical problems and the remedy for them. For example, one allegedly misleading feature of our language is that "a substantive makes us look for a thing that corresponds to it." If we are puzzled about the nature of time, Wittgenstein suggested that "it is the use of the substantive 'time' which mystifies us."[36] The substantive inclines us to think of time as a thing possessing hidden properties that we need to unearth, when in fact we just need to examine how we talk about time, and then our puzzlement will go away.

In the *Blue Book*, Wittgenstein frequently invoked the ordinary: "our ordinary use of language," "in ordinary life," "our ordinary way of expression." But what about the extraordinary? Sometimes Wittgenstein seemed beholden to the commonplace, and too quick to dismiss the unusual as if it were the impossible. Thus, in a discussion of what he called "the peculiar grammar of the word 'I,'" Wittgenstein suggested that if you say you have toothache, you cannot be mistaken about whose toothache it is. "To ask 'are you sure that it's *you* who have pains?' would be nonsensical," according to Wittgenstein. Yet there are brain injuries that can produce this "nonsensical" state of affairs. The rare condition of somatoparaphrenia may cause people to feel pain in a limb and yet say that they do not know whose pain it is.[37] So the "grammar" of our everyday talk may not be an unerring guide to what is impossible or nonsensical.

One might also question the extent to which it is "our way of expression" that is ultimately to blame for philosophical trouble. If there are misleading pictures "embedded in our language," how did they come to be there? Did Wittgenstein get to the bottom of the matter? Sraffa jotted down some queries about the *Blue Book:* "Have you found out whether these puzzles have in fact arisen out of this attitude to language, have you made sure that they did not exist before anyone took that attitude etc? And also, is it a fact that the disease is cured by your prescription? Even if this is so, you have only based it on your assertion, you have not given the evidence."[38] Sraffa presumably put these points to Wittgenstein, but there is no record of his response.

The idea that some philosophical problems and opinions arise at least in part from misunderstandings about language is as old as Western philosophy itself. Both Plato and Aristotle accused the pre-Socratic philosopher Parmenides of being led to absurd views because he was in a muddle about the verb "to be." This verb was still leading philosophers astray in the seventeenth century, according to Hobbes. In the 1870s, Nietzsche complained that a whole "philosophical mythology lies concealed in *language*."[39] Frege and Russell were the immediate precursors of Wittgenstein's focus on language, but Wittgenstein sought to go further and deeper than they did. For Frege and Russell, attention to language could bring light into some areas of philosophy; for Wittgenstein, it illuminated the whole. Whatever its limitations, his linguistic account of the nature of philosophical problems is one of the most audacious and intriguing theories in the history of the subject.

Wittgenstein filled thirty pages of his 1933 typescript with remarks about the nature of philosophy. A philosophical problem is "an awareness of the disorder in our concepts," he wrote. And a philosophical problem "always has the form: 'I simply don't know my way about.'" When he characterized philosophy in these sweeping ways, Wittgenstein seems himself to have succumbed to the "craving for generality" that he criticized. Can such a variegated subject be captured in these universal formulas? Sometimes he was more circumspect and indicated that he did not mean to generalize about all of philosophy. "Philosophy, *as we use the word* [my emphasis], is a fight against the fascination which forms of expression exert on us," he said in the *Blue Book*, in which he also conceded that his novel way of pursuing the subject was only one of the legitimate "heirs" of old-time philosophy.[40]

Wittgenstein's pronouncements on the nature of philosophy should perhaps be taken in the same spirit as his statements about religion, which tend to describe religious belief not as it is but as he would wish it to be. He wrote that "Christianity is not a doctrine, not, I mean, a theory about what has happened & will happen to the human soul, but a description of something that actually takes place in human life." For him, religion was "really a way of living, or a way of judging life." But he knew that for his Catholic friends it was something more. They accepted doctrines about a historical Jesus and the fate of their souls: "I could not possibly bring myself to believe all the things that they believe," he once remarked. Wittgenstein's descriptions of religion match only those forms of it that appealed to him. Similarly, his picture of philosophy reflected his own interests and talents. His friend von Wright believed that Wittgenstein's account of the subject was not intended as "an attempt to tell us what philosophy, once and for all, *is* but expressed what for him, in the setting of his times, it had to be."[41] Although Wittgenstein's remarks do not accurately represent the subject as a whole, some of them are apt observations on its parts. "I simply don't know my way about" nicely fits the attempts of philosophers to navigate certain puzzles. The mind-body problem and the problem of free will are two examples. In neither case is there much agreement about exactly what the question is, or what sort of thing might count as an answer to it.

One of the pupils to whom Wittgenstein dictated in the early 1930s was Francis Skinner, with whom he had his longest love affair. When he met Wittgenstein in late 1932, Skinner was a mathematics undergraduate at Trinity with an interest in philosophy, as Pinsent had been two decades earlier. Unlike Pinsent, Skinner was aware of Wittgenstein's love, and more than returned it. He more or less put aside his own work, at first in order to help Wittgenstein and then to take up whatever occupation Wittgenstein thought best for him. As a particularly promising student, Skinner was awarded a postgraduate scholarship at Trinity, but he seems to have spent the time mostly as Wittgenstein's amanuensis and sympathetic listener. There was a plan for the two men to immigrate to Russia in 1936, when Skinner's scholarship and Wittgenstein's fellowship were due to end. There they would perhaps work together on a collective farm. When this scheme came to nothing, Skinner was talked into working as an apprentice mechanic, much to the dismay of his family.

Fania Pascal, who gave Russian lessons to Wittgenstein and Skinner, and knew them throughout the 1930s, remembered

Skinner as boyish, kind, sensitive, extremely shy, and "too unselfish, too self-effacing." Wittgenstein's tone toward him was "stern, as of a judge" and she found (as did others) that Skinner was more at ease when Wittgenstein was not around. Wittgenstein could be "a holy terror and . . . a know-all," Pascal noted. She thought that he could not help much of his irascibility because "his life was made hard by excessive sensibility." Wittgenstein himself once recorded that "my mental apparatus is built in an extraordinarily complicated & delicate manner & therefore more sensitive than normal."[42]

When Wittgenstein made an exploratory visit to Russia in 1935, Skinner was too unwell to accompany him. He had suffered from osteomyelitis as a teenager, which left him with a disfigured leg that gave him recurring trouble. The purpose of the visit, Wittgenstein told Keynes, who helped to arrange it, was to discover whether he could get a suitable job in Russia. It turned out that there were Russians who were willing to employ him, but only as a professor of philosophy, not as a farmworker. This was not the only problem. He would not be able to live there, Wittgenstein announced upon his return, because "one couldn't speak one's mind. . . . It is as though one were to spend the rest of one's life in the army."[43]

Unlike that of some other Cambridge academics of the time, including a few of his friends, Wittgenstein's long-standing interest in Russia had not been sparked by politics. It may have been somewhat true that he had "sympathies with the way of life which he believes the new régime in Russia stands for," as Keynes diplomatically told the Russian ambassador. But Wittgenstein had talked with Engelmann about fleeing to Russia in 1922, mainly to escape some of the odious locals in Upper Austria, and Pascal was sure that his feelings for Russia had "more to do with Tolstoy's moral teachings, with Dostoevsky's spiritual insights, than with any political or social matters." Wittgenstein may, though, have been more forgiving of Stalin's regime than was his politically conservative brother Paul. On a concert tour of the Soviet Union in 1930, Paul declared that life in the country would have been infinitely better if the Russians had kept their tsar. Ludwig, on the other hand, told a friend in 1939 that those who accused Stalin of betraying the Russian Revolution "have no idea of the problems [he] had to deal with." This may not have been his considered opinion; it is not clear that Wittgenstein had many considered opinions about politics. Marguerite Respinger thought the subject was "too unclean" for him.[44]

In the summer of 1936, when Wittgenstein was pondering his next move, Waismann gingerly approached Gretl to ask if her brother might consider a teaching post in Vienna. She assured Waismann that it was out of the question. Waismann's overture was prompted by the fact that Schlick had just been murdered by an unstable former student, and Wittgenstein was being mooted as a possible successor. Schlick's killer, Hans Nelböck, declared in court that his victim had stolen "his love, his faith and his existence." A woman who had spurned him was, in Nelböck's mind, involved with Schlick. When he petitioned for a pardon after the German annexation of Austria, Nelböck claimed that he had acted to protect the German nation from corrupting influences. The petition was unsuccessful, but there was sympathy in some quarters for this excuse. Soon after the murder, a pseudonymous article in a Catholic journal by "Prof. Dr. Austriacus" conceded that Nelböck was a psychopath, but alleged that it was Schlick's godless and positivistic philosophy, with its "radical denial of anything metaphysical," that had driven him insane. What the tragic case exposed, according to Austriacus, was "the Jews' dangerous intellectual influence."[45] Schlick was not Jewish, though Waismann and other members of the circle were.

Wittgenstein moved back to his former house in Norway in August 1936, hoping to produce something publishable, while Skinner was left making mainscrews at the Cambridge Scientific

Instrument Company, thinking about Wittgenstein and wishing they were together. Skinner would not be happy in academic life, Wittgenstein told Pascal, and she thought that this was probably right, though he does not seem to have been content as a mechanic, either. Wittgenstein's work went sporadically well over the next seventeen months, which he spent mainly in Norway interspersed with long visits to Cambridge and Vienna. The first two-fifths of his *Philosophical Investigations* were written in this period. There were also miserable episodes of anguished introspection and idiosyncratic prayerfulness: "God let me be pious but *not* eccentric!"[46] Periods of isolation in Norway not only paid philosophical dividends but also provided the opportunity for self-examination, just as they had done in 1913–14.

The Norway manuscript that grew into Wittgenstein's *Investigations* began with an excerpt from St. Augustine's *Confessions*, in which Augustine recounted how he taught himself to speak by watching adults use names for objects. It seemed to Wittgenstein that this passage exhibited "a particular picture of the essence of human language. It is this: the words in language name objects—sentences are combinations of such names.—In this picture of language we find the roots of the following idea: Every word has a meaning. This meaning is correlated with the word. It is the object for which the word stands."[47] Wittgenstein then elaborated his own picture of the diverse functions of language, criticizing what he took to be Augustine's account and elements of his own former views in the *Tractatus*. Next he mused on the nature of philosophy as he saw it before proceeding to language-learning, with a focus on how pupils learn to follow a rule or continue a simple arithmetical series. The rest of the *Investigations*, written later in life, extended his discussion of rule-following, continued the *Blue Book*'s project of turning the mind inside out (by undermining the idea of mental privacy), and explored the activities of thinking, believing, imagining, seeing, expecting, and intending, among other things.

Wittgenstein's Norway writings of 1936–37 contained all of his most distinctive thoughts on the nature of philosophy. Philosophical problems arise when language embarks on ill-advised adventures, and the philosopher's job is to shepherd it back home. This task is not like any sort of scientific inquiry: it involves no more than describing the working of our language. Such exercises in description will somehow neutralize various forms of troublesome nonsense, and thereby secure a victory in the "battle against the bewitchment of our intelligence."

Wittgenstein insisted that his sort of inquiry "leaves everything as it is" and does not involve propounding any theses. This has puzzled commentators because his writings do appear to promote views that he wishes his readers to accept—for example, that language is more complex and diverse than the excerpt from Augustine suggests, and that our mental lives are not as intrinsically private as has been supposed. If Wittgenstein's philosophy really left everything as it is, why would one bother to read it? It seems that Wittgenstein was trying to follow in the footsteps of Boltzmann, who maintained that the most useful task for a philosopher is to correct the errors of other philosophers. As Boltzmann put it in one of his popular writings, philosophers "have done useful work in removing defective views, uncovering their mistakes and thus spreading a transition to clearer views." Wittgenstein presumably saw himself as undoing the damage caused by bad ideas rather than propounding new ones of his own. This exercise, though not quite leaving everything as it is, would merely return things to where they were before other philosophers unhelpfully moved them. Wittgenstein seems to have acknowledged as much when he wrote that what his sort of investigations achieved was the destruction of "castles in the air."[48]

After three months of writing and introspection by his fjord, Wittgenstein suddenly unburdened himself in November 1936 in a letter to a close friend, Ludwig Hänsel, whom he had met in the war: "I lied to you & several others back then during the Italian internment when I said that I was descended one quarter from Jews and three quarters from Aryans, even though it is just the other way round. This cowardly lie has burdened me for a long time & like *many* other lies I also told this one to others. Until today I did not find the strength to confess it."[49] Wittgenstein asked Hänsel to pass on this pressing news to his wife and children, and to some mutual friends and to members of the Wittgenstein family in Vienna, including all of his siblings' children. Hänsel, at first unwilling to comply, urged Wittgenstein to confess to a priest. According to the Nuremberg racial laws that were announced in Germany the year before, anyone who was at least three-quarters descended from Jews counted as a Jew. It is possible that this political development partly spurred Wittgenstein's confession, but there were plenty of other dark matters on his mind as well. After he wrote to Hänsel, he began "thinking again & again how I can & should make a full confession to everyone," he noted in his diary. Even his philosophical work was a cause for self-recrimination. In his lectures he had "cheated often" by pretending to understand something when in fact he did not. He planned to present his family with a comprehensive account of his failings when he went home to Vienna for Christmas, and wrote some letters to prepare them for this important event. Gretl wrote back that if his confessions gave him some relief, she was glad for that, but reassured him that she was just as bad a person, or worse. Skinner similarly sought to reassure Wittgenstein: "Whatever you have to tell me about yourself can't make any difference to my love for you. . . . There won't be any question of my forgiving you as I am a much worse person than you are."[50]

Pascal was one of several friends to whom he confessed in England during visits from Norway in 1937. She recalled that one admission concerned his Jewish ancestry and another was about his treatment of schoolchildren. A former Cambridge pupil to whom Wittgenstein unburdened himself in a café recalled that his reported misdeeds included: having initially been afraid to carry out an order during the war, though he did subsequently perform it; having reacted to some news as if he had not heard it before, when in fact he had; and, though this was vaguely expressed, having had some kind of sexual encounter with a woman in his youth. Pascal was wearied by Wittgenstein's lengthy enumeration of faults: "At one stage I cried out: 'What is it? You want to be perfect?' And he pulled himself up proudly, saying: 'Of *course* I want to be perfect.'"[51]

When he returned to Norway in early 1937 after a few weeks in Cambridge, Wittgenstein continued to rue his sins. Vanity and cowardice were often mentioned in his diaries: he was especially afraid that people would lose their high opinion of him. He also feared that his vanity somehow undermined the value of his work, which sometimes seemed to him to be meaningless. He yearned for Skinner but was concerned that he would not do the right thing by him. Wittgenstein felt himself to be "not *loving* enough, that is, too *egoistic.*" If he was a base egotist, then he could not hope for a peaceful death, and without that hope, he could not live peacefully, either. He did not have a pure heart: his thoughts were full of "vanity, swindle, resentment," and he asked God to guide his life.[52]

Skinner was also yearning, and thinking about their relationship. He wished they could do some sort of work together. After part of the summer spent together in Cambridge, Skinner asked whether it might help Wittgenstein's work if he came to Norway, which he did for two weeks in September. During this visit, Wittgenstein recorded in his dairy that they were sexually intimate: "Lay with him two or three times. Always at first with the feeling that it was nothing bad, *then* with shame." Although there is no sign that Wittgenstein shared Weininger's extreme disapproval of sex, he was uncomfortable with sensuality. He seems to have regarded it as a threat to purity and decency, even when nobody else was involved. Later that year, when he was alone in Norway, his diary entries include: "Masturbated in the night; then shame," "Masturbated tonight; sad but true," "Masturbated tonight. How bad is it? I think it is bad, but have no reason."[53]

Shortly before Skinner's arrival in Norway, Wittgenstein's philosophical writing turned to questions about mathematics that were related to his work on rule-following. What accounted for "the peculiar inexorability of mathematics"—the sense that one element of a series follows inevitably from its predecessor? He also pondered what he called the "hardness of the logical *must.*" This was the topic with which he had been wrestling on the same spot almost a quarter century earlier: the explanation of formal necessary truths. Before the war, he had tried to relate logical necessity to the emptiness of tautologies and to offer a somewhat analogous account of mathematics. Now he inclined to the idea that the sense of inevitability in mathematics is a product of our own practices and is thus in some sense our creation. He wanted to show that "what is called a mathematical discovery had much better be called a mathematical invention," as he later put it.[54]

For the next seven years, mathematics was the focus of a large part of Wittgenstein's writing. Critics of this work have complained that his knowledge of the subject was not extensive and that he had not kept up with developments in logic. Both charges are correct. On the other hand, he was philosophizing only about rudimentary matters involving "the calculations which we learn from ages six to fifteen"—the sort of math he had done with his village schoolchildren.[55] So perhaps his lack of technical sophistication is irrelevant. Either way, Wittgenstein's writings on mathematics have made less impact than his writings on language and on the mind.

* * *

When he went home to Vienna for Christmas in December 1937, Wittgenstein was unsure if he would ever return to Norway. He decided to go to Cambridge, though he no longer had a job there, and in January 1938 he moved into Skinner's flat above a grocer's shop, which was to be his base when in Cambridge for almost two years. Within a month, he was on the move again, to Dublin, where his friend Drury was in medical school. Wittgenstein toyed with becoming a doctor: he was particularly interested in psychiatry, and Drury arranged for him to talk to some mental patients. Wittgenstein was also trying to write philosophy, though it was not going well and he soon regretted having gone to Dublin. Also, he was worried by the situation in Austria, which was evidently about to be swallowed by Nazi Germany, and was wondering if he should go to Vienna to be with his family.

Three years earlier, he had engaged in a tangled debate with Sraffa about Austria and fascism. Wittgenstein sometimes felt the need to conduct postmortems by letter on their talks; the two men often misunderstood one another, Wittgenstein believed, because his thoughts, unlike Sraffa's, had "a certain kind of *crookedness*. . . . They are so very often doing such things like looping the loop."[56] On this occasion, the loops involved physiognomy and government: "I never said that the Austrians *couldn't* go fascist because it was incompatible with their mentality. I said that I could not imagine how this change could take place. The mistake I made was that I called fascism a kind of physiognomy & my difficulty was: how can the Austrian face change into that face which I called fascism. The answer to this should have been: Fascism isn't a face but a form of government, etc. etc."[57]

When the German army entered Austria on 12 March 1938, Wittgenstein wrote to Sraffa for advice and was urged not to go back to Vienna. He left Dublin for Cambridge, having resolved to apply for British citizenship and to resume university teaching if a job could be found. Soon he was lecturing once more, and in October he applied for the chair in philosophy from which Moore was about to retire. Meanwhile, Austria went fascist quite quickly.

Living under Nazi laws, the Wittgensteins in Vienna discovered that they were now not merely descended from Jews but were themselves Jews, and therefore subject to restrictions and about to be robbed. Paul was in an especially perilous position, as he had fathered two children by one of his piano students, Hilde Schania, who was not Jewish. This exposed him to a charge of "racial defilement." When the authorities discovered his secret family, discreetly maintained in an apartment while Paul lived in the Palais, he fled in August 1938 to Zurich and then to New York. Paul subsequently married Hilde, thus in a small way following in the footsteps of his teacher Leschetizky, who had married four of his piano students.

Gretl, an American citizen by marriage, also immigrated to New York, though not until 1940. After some initially unsuccessful attempts to obtain racial reclassification for the family, and a brief drama in which Gretl, Hermine, and Helene were detained for attempting to use passports that they did not know were fake, an apparently safe way was found for Hermine and Helene to remain in Vienna, which they both wished to do. Helene had children in Austria whose Jewish ancestry was sufficiently diluted as to present no problem; the unmarried Hermine was devoted to the home and memory of her parents and the musical life of Vienna—"only in Austria could someone play so movingly," she enthused after one concert.[58] The Wittgensteins were in a position to bargain with the Nazi authorities in Berlin because a large amount of money and gold was held in Switzerland, out of the reach of the German central bank. In effect, the family used its foreign assets to buy "half-breed" status. After an agreement was eventually reached with the bank in August 1939, their grandfather Hermann Wittgenstein was posthumously ruled to have been "German-blooded," and the Viennese authorities were instructed by Berlin to stop treating his descendants as Jews.

Paul, who had argued that Hermine and Helene ought to leave Austria, was critical of the financially complex deal. His attitude during the negotiations caused a permanent rift in the family. Ludwig also played a part in the negotiations, both diplomatically, in seeking to persuade Paul to comply, and as a director, though no longer a beneficiary, of the family's Swiss trust. At the end of his life, Ludwig wrote that he did not share his sisters' bitterness toward Paul, though he never saw his brother again after 1939. When Gretl was living in New York during the war, she went to one of Paul's concerts—"his playing has become much worse," she wrote to Ludwig—but did not make contact with him.[59]

Paul was almost proved right about the dangers that his sisters would face if they remained in Vienna. By early 1945, there were plans to send all "half-breeds" to forced-labor camps. Because of a shortage of trains, the plans had not yet been implemented by the time Soviet troops liberated the city in April 1945. It is unclear how much Hermine was aware of what was happening to most of Austria's Jews. Sometime in 1938, she wrote to Ludwig's friend Hänsel, "Until recently, I thought this time was terribly hard for Jews, but now I know that it is just as bad for other people, namely those who are principled non-Nazis."[60]

In the summer of 1938, while Paul was in flight from Vienna and other family members sought ways to undo their classification as Jews, Ludwig considered publishing selections from his notebooks. He drafted a preface in which he explained that he had given up trying to arrange his thoughts in an orderly way: "It became clear to me that the best I ever could write would just be philosophical remarks; that my thoughts soon grew lame if, against their natural inclination, I forced them along a single track.—This, however, was not unconnected with the nature of the subject itself. This subject compels us to travel through the field of thought in all directions by a host of different routes. And thus the thoughts do not naturally form a simple sequence but a complicated network."[61] In the preface, he did not do much to explain why the subject itself required him to loop the loop, which sounds like an excuse for what he could not help doing.

He was spurred to publish his remarks, he wrote, because his ideas were already in circulation, "frequently misunderstood, more or less watered down or mutilated," and he could no longer tolerate this. Wittgenstein changed his mind and did not publish anything, but there is no reason to think that what he regarded as misunderstandings would have ceased even if he had gone ahead. Diverse interpretations of his later writings have multiplied ever since his literary executors began to issue them in 1953. One reason there is much scope for disagreement about what he was trying to say is that Wittgenstein did little to spell out the connections between his remarks and the philosophical problems on which they were supposed to shed light. Readers are left to work out much for themselves, as Wittgenstein was well aware: "If this book is written as it should be, then everything I say must be easy to understand, indeed trivial; but *why* I say it will be hard to understand."[62]

"We shall obviously have to elect Wittgenstein," remarked one don when Moore's successor was being picked. In October 1939, Wittgenstein took up his new post as professor of philosophy and moved back into his old college rooms at the top of a tower in Trinity. One month earlier, the Wittgenstein family's deal with the Nazis had come into effect. Wittgenstein's worries about his relatives were therefore somewhat abated, but he had other troubles. He felt "pretty rotten in many ways, though less so now that I've moved into College," he wrote to a friend. He had not been able to do decent work for a year, partly because of "the nauseating effect political events here and elsewhere have had on me," and he seemed to be "washed up, as a researcher, for good." He did not feel qualified for his job, but he did not know what else to do. "Perhaps the war . . . may solve this problem for me," he mused, much as he had done in 1914.[63]

Britain had declared war on Germany in September; the next eight months were nicknamed "the phony war" because there was little fighting. If the war became a real one, Wittgenstein's plan was to get a job with the Red Cross. In late 1940, he completed a course in first aid, but did not start war work until October 1941, when he took a post at a London hospital. Until then, he continued teaching, not only philosophy to his Cambridge students but also some informal tutoring in science subjects to Keith Kirk, a fellow apprentice at Skinner's firm who was preparing for professional exams. Wittgenstein guiltily developed a crush on Kirk. In June 1940, he wrote in a notebook that he was "doubtful to what extent the relationship is the right one." A few months later, he spent a whole day pondering the matter, though it was only in Wittgenstein's head that the relationship was an amorous one. Like Pinsent, Kirk seems to have been unaware of the sort of feelings Wittgenstein had for him. In his biography of Wittgenstein, Ray Monk suggested that Wittgenstein's romantic affairs were conducted from a position of "emotional solipsism" and "in the splendid isolation of his own feelings."[64] Wittgenstein perhaps revealed his need for safe distances from the objects of his affection when he wrote to his last paramour that love is measured not by what a person does and feels for another when they are together, but by what he feels and does when they are apart.

On the surface, Wittgenstein and Skinner continued much as before, though living separately. They went on holiday together, and Gretl always sent love to Skinner when she wrote to her brother. Suddenly, in October 1941, Skinner was taken ill and died of polio at the age of twenty-nine. Three days after

Skinner's death, Wittgenstein requested a leave of absence from Cambridge and moved to London a week later to start work as a dispensary porter at Guy's Hospital. Full of remorse, he recorded in December that he had been "very often very unloving and in my heart unfaithful" to Skinner in the past two years. Skinner was thus added to Wittgenstein's stock of material for self-recrimination. Seven years later, he rued how "detestable" he had been to him: "I don't see how I can ever be free of this guilt."[65]

Just before Skinner fell ill Wittgenstein had been offered a job at Guy's by the philosopher Gilbert Ryle's brother, who was a doctor. He wanted a manual job in a hospital, preferably in a blitzed area, Wittgenstein told Dr. Ryle, because he felt he would die slowly if he stayed in Cambridge, and would prefer to take the chance of dying quickly somewhere. Wittgenstein's first job at Guy's was to deliver medicines from its dispensary. His manager recalled that "after working here three weeks he came and explained how we should be running the place. You see, he was a man who was used to thinking."[66]

One radiologist reckoned that Wittgenstein's sometimes awkward interactions in the hospital resulted from the fact that he wanted to have ordinary conversations with people but did not know how to conduct them. His attempts to be friendly could gauchely misfire. "There was," she said, "something very touching or innocent about him. . . . He was entirely unsophisticated." Wittgenstein did in fact know how to have relaxed and jokey conversations, but only with certain people who were often themselves unsophisticated in some way. He found such a person in the dispensary, Roy Fouracre, an easygoing, young assistant from a modest background who became a lifelong friend. In his letters to Wittgenstein after he had joined the army, Fouracre recalled the "grand time" they had together at Guy's: "I was thinking (I do think) the other day about those little boating trips we used to have and our trips to the zoo[.] I often wonder how they ever let us out once we got in." When Fouracre was in Indonesia and had apparently not received some of Wittgenstein's letters, Wittgenstein speculated that the censor "keeps them as souvenirs because they are so marvelous," and urged him to "finish your tours to South Sumatra & to Central Sumatra & take a plane (I don't mean the sort a joiner uses) & get home."[67] The heaviness of Wittgenstein's humor was one of the first things Pinsent had noticed about him in 1912. His middle sister, Helene, and her husband were among those to whom Wittgenstein regularly sported his heavy-handed light-hearted side.

After some serious conversations in the canteen at Guy's with members of a clinical research unit, Wittgenstein became involved with the team's work, studying traumatic shock (which was in those days called "wound shock"). The unit moved to a hospital in Newcastle where Wittgenstein joined them in April 1943 as a laboratory assistant. Its director, Ronald Grant, was so impressed by his contributions that he said it was a pity that Wittgenstein was a philosopher and not a physiologist. At Grant's suggestion, Wittgenstein wrote a paper about some of his experimental findings for possible submission to a medical journal, though it was never published.

When he could spare the time and was in the mood, Wittgenstein kept up his philosophical writing during his almost two and a half years in London and Newcastle. Philosophy was "the only work that's given me real satisfaction," he wrote in September to a friend. In early 1944, Wittgenstein left Newcastle and tried once more to prepare his manuscript for publication. He moved for several months to Swansea where his friend Rush Rhees was a lecturer in philosophy, and then returned to Cambridge in October 1944 to resume his duties as professor. Russell also returned to Cambridge at the same time after six years in the United States; he was now seventy-two and had been appointed to a lectureship at Trinity. But Wittgenstein had cooled toward him. "I've seen Russell and Moore," he wrote to Rhees. "Russell somehow gave me a *bad* impression. Moore is as nice as always."[68]

Wittgenstein later explained to a student that Moore lacked Russell's intellectual powers, but he did have sincerity, which Russell had lost. So it was profitable to have discussions with Moore, but not with Russell. When they occasionally met at the Moral Sciences Club, Wittgenstein was outwardly respectful toward Russell, though he told Moore that he found Russell to be "glib and superficial, though, as always, *astonishingly* quick."[69] He disparaged Russell's popular writings, especially those on ethics and politics.

Wittgenstein had fierce convictions about the sort of writing that was fitting for a serious thinker. Three years earlier, he had issued a stern warning to Moore: "I fear that you may now be walking at the edge of that cliff at the bottom of which I see lots of scientists and philosophers lying dead, Russell amongst others. My whole object in writing you was to say*: may a good spirit be with you* and keep you from getting dizzy and falling down."[70] Wittgenstein's warning was prompted by the news that Moore was to be the subject of a volume in *The Library of Living Philosophers*, a series of books in which academics criticize the work of an eminent thinker, who in turn contributes an intellectual autobiography and detailed replies to their criticisms. For Wittgenstein, such an exercise smacked of contemptible journalism. Some years earlier, he had condemned as "prostitution" another series of volumes, *Contemporary British Philosophy*.[71] At the time he made that remark, Wittgenstein did not realize that "A Defence of Common Sense," which he later said was Moore's best article, had been written for this series.

In Wittgenstein's opinion, Russell's days of serious philosophizing were over: "Russell isn't going to kill himself doing philosophy now," he said to a friend in 1946.[72] Russell was, though, still working at the subject. His interest in reasoning, which had previously focused on the inferences used in logic and mathematics, now broadened to include the patterns of argument employed in science and everyday life. In his lectures at Trinity, Russell investigated probability, analogical reasoning, causal explanation, and the invocation of postulates, among other things. These topics were the subject of his last substantial book of philosophy, *Human Knowledge: Its Scope and Limits*, which was published in 1948. But Wittgenstein was right that Russell was in the twilight of his philosophical career. Instead of killing himself at the subject, he turned instead to the problem of how to stop people killing one another. Russell devoted much of his final two decades to campaigning for nuclear disarmament and protesting against the Vietnam War.

Russell thought that Wittgenstein had taken a wrong turn in philosophy, though he did not say so in print until after Wittgenstein's death in 1951. One admirer of Russell's who shared this opinion, and was eager to confront Wittgenstein, was Karl Popper, a philosopher with a growing reputation in the philosophy of science and in political theory who addressed the Moral Sciences Club in October 1946. This meeting of the club later became famous for an incident that was not even a storm in a teacup.

Popper was a fellow emigré from Vienna, thirteen years younger than Wittgenstein. It is probably because Popper was so proud and combative that Schlick, who had been an examiner of his doctoral dissertation in 1928, did not invite him to join his circle. Wittgenstein was half joking when he claimed to have founded logical positivism, but Popper was entirely serious when he claimed to be the man who had killed it. Popper maintained not only that he had refuted the views of the Vienna Circle and exposed flaws in the *Tractatus*, but also that he had solved various philosophical problems. He therefore did not take kindly to the idea that there were really no such problems to solve, just linguistic misunderstandings. He went to Cambridge "hoping to provoke Wittgenstein" on the matter, as he admitted in his autobiography.[73]

In his Cambridge talk, Popper criticized what he called Wittgenstein's "Linguistic Philosophy," claiming that it dealt only with preliminary matters and never got round to serious ones.[74] According to Popper, in an account that was written more than two decades after the event:

> Wittgenstein jumped up . . . and spoke at length about puzzles and the nonexistence of philosophical problems. . . . I interrupted him, giving a list I had prepared of philosophical problems, such as: Do we know things through our senses?, Do we obtain our knowledge by induction? These Wittgenstein dismissed as being logical rather than philosophical. I then referred to the problem whether potential or perhaps even actual infinities exist, a problem he dismissed as mathematical. . . . I then mentioned moral problems and the problem of the validity of moral rules. At that point Wittgenstein, who was sitting near the fire and had been nervously playing with the poker, which he sometimes used like a conductor's baton to emphasize his assertions, challenged me: "Give an example of a moral rule!" I replied: "Not to threaten visiting lecturers with pokers." Whereupon Wittgenstein, in a rage, threw the poker down and stormed out of the room, banging the door behind him.[75]

Wittgenstein's only comment about the supposed drama, made a few days afterward, was that it had been a bad meeting "in which an ass, Dr Popper from London, talked more mushy rubbish than I've heard for a long time."[76] Long after the event, witnesses gave conflicting accounts of what had happened. Popper wrote that his remark about threats to visiting lecturers had been merely a joke, so it is reasonable to assume that no poker was wielded with intent. On the other hand, Wittgenstein's way with his walking stick had led to misunderstanding in the past. Nine years earlier, he had been puzzled by the sudden frostiness of a female friend in Skjolden; it emerged that she thought he had threatened her with his stick. Wittgenstein was aghast because his friendly tap had been meant affectionately.

Wittgenstein had other troubles on his mind when Popper came to provoke him. He was often depressed, and had been thinking all year about resigning his chair, though he was not sure that this would help. A few weeks after Popper's talk, Wittgenstein wrote in a notebook that "I foresee a bad end to my life. Loneliness, perhaps madness. My lectures are going well, they will never go better. But what effect do they have? Am I helping anyone?" He sometimes felt that "trying to do philosophy at a university is a completely hopeless job." And not all of his problems were prompted by work. Something else had gripped him "almost like a madness" for the past nine months, Wittgenstein wrote in July 1946. This was his love affair with Ben Richards, a Cambridge graduate in natural sciences who had come to one of his lectures. "The *one* thing that my love for B. has done for me," Wittgenstein wrote in a notebook, is to have "driven the paltry sorrows of my position and my work into the background, at least for a while."[77]

Everyone with whom Wittgenstein is known to have fallen in love was aged between twenty and twenty-two when he fell for them. The gap in ages between him and his current beloved therefore grew steadily, from three years in the case of David Pinsent in 1912 to thirty-five years in the case of Ben Richards in 1945. Wittgenstein was sure that Richards's feelings for him could not last. If no letter came, he was tormented by the thought that Richards had left him or was thinking of doing so. His ability to philosophize depended precariously on the state of their relationship: "I couldn't be writing like this now if I hadn't spent the last 2 weeks with B.," Wittgenstein noted in early October

1946, when work was going well. Seven weeks later, he berated himself: "Can you not be happy without his love? . . . You mustn't always be waiting for letters that don't come."[78]

But Richards's feelings for Wittgenstein did last. In the final years of his life, Wittgenstein delighted in holidays, music, botany, and books together with the gentle, shy, and good-looking Richards. "You are at the background of *all* my happiness," Wittgenstein wrote to him in one of his last letters.[79] The two men were mostly apart and never lived together. Richards's replies to Wittgenstein's sometimes avuncular and often passionate correspondence were devotedly affectionate, and always less fraught than Skinner's letters had sometimes been. Wittgenstein died holding Richards's hand.

When Richards was a medical student and living at the family home in Ickenham, a suburb of northwest London, Wittgenstein visited several times, and got to know Richards's mother, who had heard all about him in 1912 from her admirer Békássy—a coincidental reconnection with the extended Bloomsbury circle of his earliest Cambridge years (see chapter 4). After Wittgenstein's death, Richards spent most of his career as a rheumatologist, played the viol in early-music consorts, married at the age of fifty-two, and kept up an interest in the sciences and in philosophy. In the 1970s, he took university courses in, among other things, the philosophy of Wittgenstein.

Since returning to Cambridge in 1929, Wittgenstein had filled thousands of pages of manuscripts and typescripts, yet still had no new book to publish. In the summer of 1947, he decided to try once more to get something finished, and applied for one term of sabbatical leave. He soon realized that this would not be enough time, and resigned his professorship in October 1947, just after returning from a visit to Vienna.

He had not been home for eight years. "It's sad that we have to live so completely cut off from one another," he had written to Helene the previous year.[80] There was talk of Hermine moving into the house that he had built for Gretl, an idea that pleased him because he wanted someone from the family to live there. Gretl eventually moved back from New York and lived in it herself. Wittgenstein's meticulously conceived modern palace had been used as stables by the Russian army in 1945. It needed renovation, and its contents were mostly lost. Gretl joked that if he wanted to earn money, he could perhaps design some more furniture for it.

Wittgenstein never finished his *Philosophical Investigations* or any other new work, but the urge to think and write about philosophy continued to drive him until the end of his life. There was no more time for anything else. The first year and a half of his retirement was spent mostly in Ireland, at a guesthouse near the east coast, then a cottage on the west coast, then Dublin, with visits to Vienna, Cambridge, Oxford, and Ickenham to see Richards. In 1949, he spent three months in Ithaca, New York, staying with his friend and former pupil Norman Malcolm, and thereafter mostly lodged with other former pupils in Cambridge and Oxford, trying to write whenever his health and mood permitted.

When asked why he had retired, Wittgenstein said it was not only because he wanted to write, but also because his teaching had not done much good. There were "only two or three of my students about whom I can say, I do not know I have done them any harm." He had told his pupils to think for themselves and not to bother with old books by other people. Yet he came to realize that his teaching usually did not elicit independent thinking but rather imitations of himself. And he did not want to be imitated, especially not by "those who publish articles in philosophical journals." He mused enigmatically that "a change in the way we live, making all these [philosophical] questions superfluous" might be more desirable than any sort of continuation of his work by others.[81]

One of the pupils whom Wittgenstein felt he had not harmed was his Finnish student von Wright, a philosopher whose writings show no trace of Wittgenstein's mannerisms, except in one early essay. Von Wright worked in a conventional manner, formulating theories and advancing arguments for them, at first mainly on the topics of probable inference and some applications of logic. He wrote that Wittgenstein influenced his intellectual development more than anyone else, but "his *style* of thought is so different from my own. I admire it but cannot (even try to) imitate it."[82] Wittgenstein recommended von Wright as his successor, and he was duly elected professor of philosophy at Cambridge at the age of thirty-two.

"Cambridge is a dangerous place," Wittgenstein wrote to him from Ireland in February 1948. "Will you become superficial? smooth? If you don't, you will have to suffer terribly." For some of his time in Ireland, Wittgenstein was himself suffering. At first, work went well, though he wrote to Malcolm that he had "occasional queer states of nervous instability about which I'll only say that they're rotten while they last, and teach one to pray." In March, he was severely depressed for several weeks and told von Wright that he often thought he was on the road to insanity. But his work was sporadically progressing, and he wrote to Richards that he had become "*very* much clearer about the problems that baffled me for years."[83]

One thing that reliably lifted Wittgenstein's spirits in Ireland was American pulp-fiction magazines, which Malcolm mailed to him. Wittgenstein favorably contrasted these with the philosophical journal *Mind:* "If philosophy has anything to do with wisdom there's certainly not a grain of that in *Mind,* and quite often a grain in the detective stories." Later in the year, living in Dublin, there was also the addictive distraction of the cinema. "I wish I could cut down on it," he wrote to Richards. Wittgenstein enjoyed American films best—he once wrote that he had often "drawn a lesson from a foolish American film"—and he enthused to Richards about *The Mating of Millie*, a new romantic comedy about a good-hearted employee of a department store. When he was planning a journey to New York the next year, he joked to Malcolm that perhaps "like in the films, I'll find a beautiful girl whom I meet on the boat and who will help me."[84]

The hotel in Dublin where Wittgenstein mostly lived from October 1948 until June 1949 was close to the hospital where Drury worked, and not far from the National Botanic Gardens, from which Wittgenstein sometimes stole leaves and blossoms to send to Richards. He often took his notebook and worked in the warmth of its Great Palm House, where a plaque now commemorates the spot on which he supposedly sat. Wittgenstein also regularly went to the nearby zoo, where he made one of his throwaway remarks on a visit with Drury, which Drury duly recorded: "I have always thought that Darwin was wrong: his theory doesn't account for all this variety of species. It hasn't the necessary multiplicity."[85]

In early 1949, Wittgenstein received distressing reports from Vienna about his sister Hermine, who had been diagnosed with cancer the previous year. She was now dying, he was told, which was a great loss for him, he wrote. "All around me, the roots on which my life depend are being severed. My soul is full of pain."[86] He regarded Hermine as the deepest of his siblings. The news of her demise was, though, premature; she lived on for another year. By the time Wittgenstein went to visit her in April, his own health was failing. When he returned from Vienna in May, he was diagnosed with a severe form of anemia, but rallied enough to go ahead with his American trip, embarking in late July.

Malcolm was surprised by Wittgenstein's vigor as he strode off the ship with his habitual rucksack. On their long train journey to upstate New York, where Malcolm taught at Cornell University, Wittgenstein gave one of his whistled virtuoso performances, of parts of Beethoven's Seventh Symphony. According to Malcolm, his guest's health was fairly good for the first six weeks or so, but in September he was so unwell that he spent two days in the hospital for tests. Wittgenstein was relieved when the doctors found nothing because he wanted to die in Europe, not in America, where the people were nice, but for the most part very foreign to him. In a faint echo of his father's paean to American industry, he wrote to Rhees that the only thing he really enjoyed there was "the engineering; that's superb. I like to see American machines."[87]

Wittgenstein hoped to do some work, he told Richards at the start of his stay. He was writing new material, and some of the discussions he had with Malcolm and others at Cornell were, in Wittgenstein's judgment, not too bad. To some of the graduate students, Wittgenstein's performance at a meeting of the Cornell Philosophy Club was thrilling. William Gass, who became a novelist, wrote that it was "the most important intellectual experience of my life, yet it was an experience almost wholly without content, for it was very plainly not just what the old man said that was so moving, it was almost entirely the way in which he said it, the total naked absorption of the mind in its problem." Another student recorded that the substance of what Wittgenstein said was forgettable, but the man himself seemed to shine with an uncanny concentration and dedication to truth.[88]

The unusual intensity of Wittgenstein's thinking was revealed in a different way in a letter he wrote to Richards at the end of his stay in America. He was shocked to learn that Richards was letting his beard grow, and tried to explain why doing such a thing for no apparent reason was "a *wanton* way of playing about with something which, if you love somebody, is not quite your own." Wittgenstein thought about Richards all the time, as he often told him, and these thoughts were essential to his well-being. His point was not an aesthetic one, he insisted: "You know that I have always looked at your face with delight. When I felt bad & depressed I looked forward to seeing it, &

when I saw it I felt good again. . . . Your face is something *sacred* to the person who loves you & if you play about with it, you *play* with something that's sacred to me—I mean every word of this."[89]

A month after his return to England, while staying in Cambridge with von Wright, Wittgenstein was diagnosed with prostate cancer that had spread to his bone marrow. Hormone treatment might enable him to live on for years, he was told. His Cambridge doctor Edward Bevan said he might even be able to work again. Wittgenstein was skeptical about this, but Bevan was proved right.

By late December, Wittgenstein was strong enough to travel to Vienna for what was certain to be Hermine's last Christmas, and he requested his old room in the Palais. Letters written during the three months he stayed in Vienna mostly reported that his health was pretty good, and he claimed to be getting fat on the fine food with which he was pampered. All three of Wittgenstein's sisters were in Vienna, and the Palais resounded with music again, though less grandly than in their parents' time. Hermine was not always coherent when awake, Wittgenstein wrote to Rhees, but she listened intently to the sometimes "heavenly" piano playing of Koder, Wittgenstein's friend from his schoolmastering days, who performed duets with Helene.[90]

Wittgenstein's pupil Anscombe was also in Vienna, to improve her German so that she could one day translate his *Investigations.* Although he did not envisage finishing the book, he was willing for it to appear after his death. He was now writing about something else—"not very much & not very well, but I'm glad I can do it at all." The topic was color: Wittgenstein had picked up Goethe's book on the subject, which he found partly absurd but also stimulating. He was interested to hear from Anscombe and other friends about Ryle's book *The Concept of Mind*, which had recently been published. He was told that it was "partly based on my ideas, of course without mentioning me, & was very bad & disagreeable to read," Wittgenstein wrote to Richards.[91]

Hermine died in early February, and Wittgenstein returned to England in the last week of March 1950, staying for a few weeks in Cambridge with von Wright, and then with Anscombe in Oxford, where he lived for most of nine months, writing whenever he could about certainty, color, and the mind. In October 1950, he returned to his old house in Skjolden for a month's holiday with Richards. Although he did not manage to get any work done, he was determined to keep trying, and booked a return to Skjolden at the end of the year, intending to write there alone.

Wittgenstein, not well enough to make another trip to Norway, remained at Anscombe's in Oxford, where in January 1951 he had a visitor from the Rockefeller Foundation, Chadbourne Gilpatric, who described the encounter in a memo:

> Wittgenstein . . . is obviously a very sick man. In appearance and manner of expression, he makes a powerful impression. His face has an ascetic leanness, and his skin is remarkably fair with a kind of beauty most women would envy. His eyes dominate and control your attention. He speaks with great simplicity and compelling earnestness. At once you sense his intellectual power and moral force. . . . He would say nothing about recent lines of thought because, as he said, he was bitterly dissatisfied with many attempts at formulation in the last two years. In response to a direct question about likelihood of finishing his work in book form—in progress for twenty years—he said he was no longer able to work and expected he never could again. He was firm in saying that he would accept no help from [the Rockefeller Foundation] or any other agency because he did not deserve it.[92]

There was no point in printing his unpolished manuscripts, Wittgenstein told Gilpatric: "But see, I write one sentence, and then I write another—just the opposite. And which shall stand?" After his death, Wittgenstein's literary executors decided that quite a lot of his work ought nonetheless to be published, though Anscombe, who was one of them, issued a warning that has not been much heeded by expositors. After the *Tractatus*, she insisted, "he was constantly enquiring; some things he was pretty sure of, but much was in a state of enquiry. I therefore deprecate attempts to expound Wittgenstein's thought as a finished thing."[93]

Wittgenstein once told Rhees that he would dry up if he did not revisit and revise his opinions now and then. In 1944, they had debated "the relations of grammatical propositions and empirical propositions," Rhees reported, and Wittgenstein "was working with the idea that the division between them was not a sharp one, and that his own earlier suggestions about this had been wrong or misleading."[94] This division was a crucial element in Wittgenstein's thought. Grammatical propositions, in his special sense of the term, express rules for the correct use of an expression, and "correct" here roughly means "not philosophically misleading." Consider, for example, his treatment of the philosophical thesis that people know only their own thoughts and not those of others. Wittgenstein maintained that this was in a sense the wrong way round. We can know what other people are thinking by what they say and do; but knowing what we ourselves are thinking is very different from other sorts of knowledge, or so he claimed. It is not, for instance, like knowing how much money we have in the bank, or what clothes we are wearing, because knowledge of our own thoughts is not based on evidence in the same way. He expressed this point somewhat paradoxically:

> It is correct to say "I know what you are thinking," and wrong to say "I know what I am thinking."
>
> (A whole cloud of philosophy condenses into a drop of grammar.)[95]

A "grammatical" truth, in Wittgenstein's sense, thus encapsulates the result of a philosophical inquiry. And because philosophical inquiries were, for Wittgenstein, sharply different from scientific or empirical ones, any blurring of the boundary between empirical and "grammatical" propositions threatens to undermine the wall he erected between science and philosophy. Although Wittgenstein does not seem to have pursued these tentative revisionary thoughts very far, one commentator has noticed that his writings and lectures in the 1940s show that his views on the matter were evolving.[96]

One month after Gilpatric's visit, Wittgenstein moved to Cambridge for a course of X-ray treatment, staying with Dr. Bevan and his wife, Joan. He intended to return to Oxford, but was not well enough to do so, and died twelve weeks later in the Bevans' house, which was named Storey's End. In late February, after a month at Storey's End, Wittgenstein wrote to Richards that he did not think he would ever be able to work again. At around the same time, he decided to stop taking the hormone he had been prescribed, and three weeks later found to his astonishment that his ability to work had returned: "I can still think. I'd never have expected that to happen again. But let me not crow," he wrote to Richards.[97] Wittgenstein was enthused by his progress: he was going to work as never before, he told Joan Bevan.

His writings at the time were mainly about knowledge and what can be doubted. The final remarks in his notebook, written on the day before he lost consciousness for the last time, consider the possibility that one might be dreaming:

> If someone believes that he has flown from America to England in the last few days, then, I believe, he cannot be making a *mistake*.
>
> And just the same if someone says that he is at this moment sitting at a table and writing.
>
> "But even if in such cases I can't be mistaken, isn't it possible that I am drugged?" If I am and if the drug has taken away

> my consciousness, then I am not now really talking and thinking. I cannot seriously suppose that I am at this moment dreaming. Someone who, dreaming, says "I am dreaming," even if he speaks audibly in doing so, is no more right than if he said in his dream "it is raining," while it was in fact raining. Even if his dream were actually connected with the noise of the rain.[98]

In his last weeks, Wittgenstein was so keen on a nonphilosophical book he was reading that he did something that made him sheepishly joke to Richards about being in his second childhood—"or is it still the first?"[99] He had written to Brigadier Desmond Young, an author he did not know, to tell him how much he had admired his *Rommel: The Desert Fox*, a best-selling biography of the German field marshal that controversially portrayed Rommel as something of a hero. What Wittgenstein particularly liked about the book, as he explained in his fulsome praise to several friends, was that the author wrote decently about a man who was an enemy in war. Decency in war was a topic about which Wittgenstein had strong feelings. He was scathing about the authorities at King's College, Cambridge, who had placed a memorial plaque to the Hungarian Békássy a safe distance away from the remembrance to other fallen Kingsmen who had fought on the right side.

Another bit of reading that exercised Wittgenstein in his last weeks was a magazine review of two philosophy books, which especially irked him because it "praised Waismann for a remark which comes *straight* from me." One of the books was a collection of essays by philosophers (including Ryle) who, the reviewer wrote, "derive their creed from the great Austrian philosopher Wittgenstein." In letters to his friends about the review, the great Austrian condemned all these philosophers as charlatans and wished that someone would "debunk these humbugs."[100]

Wittgenstein was in a lighter mood when he wrote to Helene in Vienna on musical matters. He had read about a new piano recording of a Bach concerto for three keyboards, he told her, and proposed to go to a shop to find out if it was any good. It turned out to be wonderful—apart from one passage—and he sent her a copy, telling her, in the silly manner that he reserved for this one of his sisters, that he must thank himself very warmly for doing so, and also thank himself for asking her to send him a small reproduction of Hermine's drawing of Josef Labor, the Palais Wittgenstein's house composer from the old days.

Joan Bevan and Wittgenstein used to walk to a nearby pub in the evenings: "We always ordered 2 ports," she recalled, "one I drank and the other one he poured with great amusement into the Aspidistra plant." After one such jaunt, on the day after his sixty-second birthday, Wittgenstein fell severely ill and was told by Dr. Bevan that he would not live much longer. The next day, the Bevans informed him that some of his close friends would arrive on the following day, 29 April. "Tell them I've had a wonderful life," he said.[101]

Death had caught him at a good moment. In his final weeks, Wittgenstein felt himself to be working better than he had done for years, and he was luxuriating in the love of Richards, who had recently written to say "I miss you terribly." Earlier in April, Wittgenstein told Richards, "You have given me happiness & joy which I never deserved & made my life different *altogether* from what it would have been without you. . . . *I love you always* & think of you all the time."[102]

In their summations of his life, many of those who knew Wittgenstein did not make it sound wonderful. His outlook "was typically one of gloom," according to von Wright. "I know his life to have been one of fulfilment, yet he seems to me a tragic character," wrote Pascal. Malcolm was "inclined to believe that his life was fiercely unhappy."[103] Wittgenstein's private writings support this dismal conclusion to some extent, especially when they expressed his feelings of unworthiness, which were so harrowing that they drove him into the arms of a God in whom he did not really believe. Given Karl Wittgenstein's disappointed expectations of his sons, perhaps one need not look far from home for a glimpse of Ludwig's God as "fearful judge."

Yet Malcolm had second thoughts about his verdict on Wittgenstein's life. There were two matters he had overlooked when he called it unhappy, he later wrote. For one thing, Wittgenstein had enjoyed many rewarding friendships. For another, his work had been a source of recurring delight, even if he often complained about it. As Wittgenstein himself once wrote, "The joy I take in my thoughts (philosophical thoughts) is the joy of my own strange life. Is that *joie de vivre?*"[104]

In 1929, while he was writing in a notebook about mathematics, Wittgenstein had paused to reflect on himself because Marguerite Respinger no longer wanted to kiss him. "My life is very strange!" he wrote in his simple code. "I don't know how bright or how dark it is. It is, as it were, half bright, half dark."[105]

The contrasts in Wittgenstein's nature were sharp and vividly on display. His own "stream of life" was a turbulent confluence, and his soul, as he once privately recorded, "is more naked than that of most people." Some of Wittgenstein's incongruities were stark but trifling failures to practice what he preached. Lettice Ramsey remarked that he "could not bear gossip, but was a great gossip himself," and he excoriated Malcolm for a remark about "national character" yet himself frequently stereotyped the English. Other contrasts ran deeper. Frances Partridge, a Bloomsbury friend of the Ramseys, found herself "brooding over the contradictions in Wittgenstein's character." His face "habitually bore an expression of concentrated seriousness and pessimism," Partridge wrote in a memoir, "yet in mixed company his conversation was often trivial in the extreme." She noted his fondness for simple pleasures such as funfairs. Some people rarely or never saw the trivial Wittgenstein, as he showed different faces to different people. Malcolm "could hardly conceive of him laughing to the point of tears," but Engelmann described an occasion on which Wittgenstein did exactly that, and "literally rolled on the carpet." One Cambridge philosopher remarked on the fact that Wittgenstein knew no intermediate state between "high and concentrated seriousness and rather simple and sometimes almost crudely 'low-brow' interludes."[106] It was all fierceness or funfairs.

On the whole, it was philosophers who were likelier to be subjected to Wittgenstein's harsher moods. Life went more swimmingly when work was far from his mind. One pupil, Alice Ambrose, suffered his wrath when she claimed in print to have been "guided throughout by certain suggestions made by Dr Ludwig Wittgenstein." As usual, he was furious to see a second-hand account of his ideas. Unusually for a pupil of Wittgenstein's, Ambrose stood up to him and told him that he was a self-centered bully. "And yet," she recounted to a friend, "there is a very great deal in him to love."[107]

Drury regarded Wittgenstein as "the most warm-hearted, generous, and loyal friend anyone could wish to have." Fifteen years after Wittgenstein's death, Dr. Bevan wrote that he had been "a great and a good man, above all . . . honest, humble, unafraid and grateful." Wittgenstein's confessions of cowardice and dishonesty were indeed largely unconvincing. His supposed humility is a less straightforward matter. He had, after all, claimed in his twenties to have found the final solution to the problems of philosophy. The "extraordinary definiteness" of the young Wittgenstein's manner, which struck a fellow prisoner of war who met him in 1919, was still there in later life. "Whatever you said, you said with such tremendous vigor and conviction, that I was always tempted to believe it without further ado," a former Cambridge pupil told him.[108] On the other hand, when Wittgenstein held forth about philosophy, his pronouncements were punctuated with groans and expressions of doubt. His charismatic gift was to be halting, self-deprecating, and imperious all at the same time.

7

A Head Full of Question Marks

A FEW WEEKS after Wittgenstein's death, Ryle told the BBC's listeners that his erstwhile friend "made our generation of philosophers self-conscious about philosophy itself." Philosophers were now perhaps slightly neurotic about their calling, Ryle said. Yet Wittgenstein had usefully taught them to be more careful with their tools. In particular, they had learned to pay attention to "what can and cannot be said."[1]

What Russell had to say about the legacy of his former protégé was at first guarded. Writing in *Mind* later that year, he recorded that getting to know Wittgenstein was "one of the most exciting intellectual adventures of my life," but noted that they had become intellectually estranged, and said nothing about Wittgenstein's ideas after the *Tractatus.* Two years later, naming no names, Russell published a satirical attack on what he described as the most influential school of philosophical thought in Britain. This school discussed "what silly people mean when they say silly things," according to Russell.[2] It sought to clarify questions, but had no interest in answering them.

In 1956, then in his mid-eighties, Russell identified the target of his ridicule: the philosophers who were influenced by Wittgenstein's *Philosophical Investigations*, which had been published in 1953. A review in *Mind* by a young Oxford philosopher, P. F. Strawson, had judged that the *Investigations* was valuable above all as a "model of philosophical method" and that it would "consolidate the philosophical revolution for which, more than anyone else, its author was responsible." But Russell could find nothing of interest in the book. The earlier Wittgenstein had been addicted to intense thinking about important problems, Russell wrote, but the later one "seems to have grown tired of serious thinking and to have invented a doctrine which would make such an activity unnecessary." That was going too far, as Russell seems to have realized. "I suppose I am perhaps being unfair," he said a few months later to a friend, after complaining that philosophers were now lazy and ignorant. "It is very hard to reconcile oneself to the idea that one's chief work—and one's final conclusions—may be out of date." Russell had been eclipsed. As he remarked in a radio talk, Wittgenstein had begun as his pupil but "ended as my supplanter at both Oxford and Cambridge."[3]

Two decades later, Wittgenstein was himself falling out of fashion in universities. His heyday lasted until the 1970s, according to Wittgensteinians, who began in the 1980s to rue the decline of his influence. "Wittgensteinian philosophy . . . has not made progress and some of the philosophical gains we owe to Wittgenstein seem in danger of being lost," wrote one eminent Oxford philosopher, Anthony Kenny, in 1984.[4] Wittgenstein said that he did not want to be copied by professional philosophers, and by the last two decades of the twentieth century, he no longer much was, though he enjoys some celebrity in the wider world as a quotably enigmatic sage. Academic philosophers still pay him more lip service than they do Russell, and they discuss his work more often than Russell's. But they generally conduct their business in Russell's way, not in Wittgenstein's. That is, they are for the most part willing to draw on findings from other disciplines; they do not tend to regard philosophical problems as mere muddles; and they try to adopt the collaborative and cautious approach of scientists, just as Russell had urged them to do.

Wittgenstein declared that philosophy is "not a body of doctrine but an activity."[5] It does not add to the stock of knowledge, but clarifies what we already possess. This was his answer to the nineteenth-century question that had been addressed by Boltzmann: What, if anything, does the march of encroaching science leave for philosophy to do?

Russell was not content with the idea that philosophy serves only to clarify. Yet he would happily have agreed that there is no such thing as a distinctively philosophical body of doctrine. For Russell, this was because of the shifting boundaries between disciplines. As he had put it in 1912: "As soon as definite knowledge concerning any subject becomes possible, this subject ceases to be called philosophy." Russell usually avoided precise definitions of philosophy. In his view, it had no special subject matter or method but was just the name for an "unusually obstinate" form of intellectual curiosity.[6] It sought a consistent overview of things while ignoring disciplinary boundaries and considerations of practical utility. According to this conception of the subject, philosophers are like small children, who press all manner of questions with tiresome insistence until they learn to become unphilosophical.

Wittgenstein recognized that tenacious curiosity was a distinguishing trait of philosophy. Late in life, he said that a philosopher is "someone with a head full of question marks." Russell told a story about his pupil's first weeks in Cambridge: "While I was still doubtful as to his ability, I asked G. E. Moore for his opinion. Moore replied, 'I think very well of him indeed.' When I enquired the reason for his opinion, he said that it was because Wittgenstein was the only man who looked puzzled at his lectures."[7] Wittgenstein had the gift of being puzzled in fresh and idiosyncratic ways. He saw things "as if for the first time," as the admiring Waismann once put it.[8] This ability to inspect familiar things from unfamiliar angles gives his work a value that does not stand or fall with his views about the nature of philosophy. One may look askance at his notion that philosophical problems are linguistic confusions, yet still find insights in his treatments of particular topics, such as the nature of mental states, the many functions of language, or the dangers of overgeneralization.

The philosophical methods employed in this age of airplanes do not now look very different from the methods that were used in the age of the horse and cart. Philosophy has always flourished in heads full of question marks, and Wittgenstein's work was not an end to traditional philosophizing but a highly personal continuation of it. When he knew that he did not have long to live, he said, "I never find myself thinking about a 'future life.' All my interest is still on this life and the writing I am still able to do."[9] For all his restlessness, Wittgenstein had in the end found his métier, even if he did sometimes think that he would rather have composed a melody.

CHRONOLOGY

1889	Ludwig Wittgenstein born in Vienna on 26 April.
1903	Attends first school, age fourteen.
1906	Engineering studies in Berlin.
1908	Aeronautical studies in Manchester.
1912	Admitted to Trinity College, Cambridge.
1913	Death of father, Karl Wittgenstein, on 20 January. Moves to Norway in October.
1914	Military service starting in August.
1918	Finishes *Tractatus Logico-Philosophicus* in August. Taken prisoner of war by Italians in November.
1919	Released from captivity in August. Relinquishes his fortune.
1920–26	Schoolteacher in Austria.
1922	*Tractatus* published in *Annalen der Naturphiloso-phie* (issue dated 1921), and as a bilingual English-German book.

1926	Death of mother, Poldy Wittgenstein, on 3 June. Begins architectural work on house for his sister Gretl in Vienna.
1929	Returns to Cambridge. Granted PhD in June, age forty.
1930–36	Teaches in Cambridge. Moves to Norway in August 1936.
1938	Returns to Cambridge in January. Germany annexes Austria in March.
1939	Elected professor of philosophy at Cambridge. Becomes British citizen.
1941–44	War work at hospitals in London and Newcastle.
1944	Resumes professorship in October.
1947	Resigns professorship, and leaves Cambridge in December.
1948–49	Mainly in Ireland until June 1949.
1949	Visit to the United States. Diagnosed with cancer in November. Last visit to Vienna in December.
1950	Mainly in Oxford from April. Last visit to Norway in October.
1951	Moves to his doctor's house in Cambridge in February. Dies on 29 April, three days after his sixty-second birthday.

FAMILY TREE

Hermann Wittgenstein
(1802–1878)
=
Fanny Figdor
(1814–1890)
five earlier children
five later children
Karl Wittgenstein
(1847–1913)
=
Leopoldine Kalmus
(1850–1926)
Hermine
(1874–1950)
Dora
(1876–1876)
Hans
(1877–1902)
Kurt
(1878–1918)
Helene
(1879–1956)
Rudi
(1881–1904)
Gretl
(1882–1958)
Paul
(1887–1961)
Ludwig
(1889–1951)

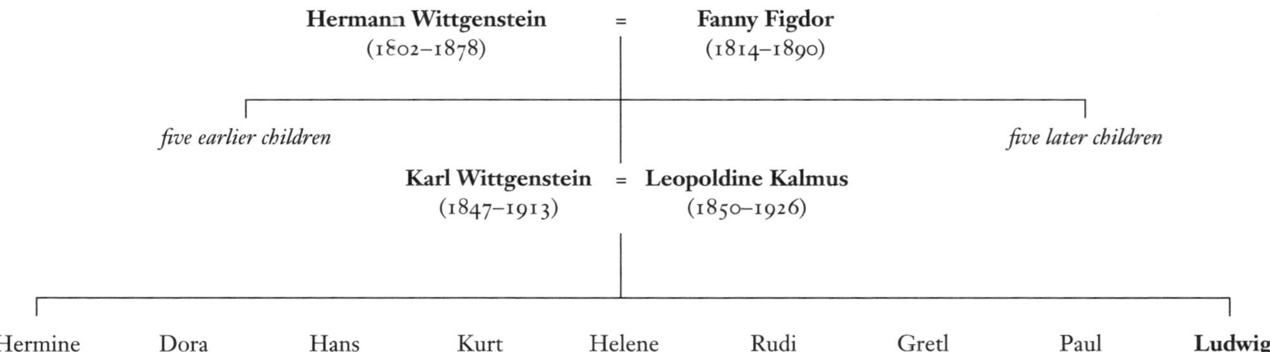

NOTES

Abbreviations

B&BB	Ludwig Wittgenstein, *The Blue and Brown Books* (Oxford: Blackwell, 1958)
C&V	Ludwig Wittgenstein, *Culture and Value*, rev. ed., ed. G. H. von Wright (Oxford: Blackwell, 1998)
CPBR	*The Collected Papers of Bertrand Russell*, vol. 6: *Logical and Philosophical Papers, 1909–1913*, ed. John Slater (London: Routledge, 1992)
DG	Ray Monk, *Ludwig Wittgenstein: The Duty of Genius* (London: Jonathan Cape, 1990)
DP	*A Portrait of Wittgenstein as a Young Man, from the Diary of David Hume Pinsent, 1912–14*, ed. G. H. von Wright (Oxford: Blackwell, 1990)
FE	Hermine Wittgenstein, *Familienerinnerungen*, ed. Ilsa Somavilla (Innsbruck-Vienna: Haymon, 2015)
GBW	*Wittgenstein: Gesamtbriefwechsel*, 2nd release (Inns-

	brucker Electronic Edition, InteLex Corporation, 2013)
LFLW	Paul Engelmann, *Letters from Ludwig Wittgenstein with a Memoir*, trans. L. Furtmueller (Oxford: Blackwell, 1967)
LW	Ludwig Wittgenstein
LWAM	Norman Malcolm, *Ludwig Wittgenstein: A Memoir*, 2nd ed. (Oxford: Oxford University Press, 1984)
MS	Manuscript from Wittgenstein's *Nachlass*, Bergen Nachlass Edition, http://www.wittgensteinsource.org/
MT	*Movements of Thought: Ludwig Wittgenstein's Diary, 1930–1932 and 1946–1937*, ed. James C. Klagge and Alfred Nordmann (London: Rowman & Littlefield, 2023)
NB	Ludwig Wittgenstein, *Notebooks, 1914–16*, 2nd ed., ed. G. H. von Wright and G. E. M. Anscombe (Oxford: Blackwell, 1979)
OLT	*On Last Things: A Translation of Weininger's Über die letzten Dinge (1904/1907)*, trans. Steven Burns (New York: Edwin Mellen, 2001)
ONB	Ludwig Wittgenstein–Ben Richards Correspondence, Österreichische Nationalbibliothek, Vienna. Transcriptions are my own. (These letters are due to be published as a book by Bloomsbury Academic, edited by Alfred Schmidt and Gabriel Citron.)
PI	Ludwig Wittgenstein, *Philosophical Investigations*, rev. 4th ed., trans. G. E. M. Anscombe, P. M. S. Hacker, and Joachim Schulte (Oxford: Wiley Blackwell, 2009)
PO	Ludwig Wittgenstein, *Philosophical Occasions*, ed. James Klagge and Alfred Nordmann (Indianapolis: Hackett, 1993)
POW	*Portraits of Wittgenstein*, 2nd ed., ed. F. A. Flowers III and Ian Ground (London: Bloomsbury Academic, 2016)
S&C	Otto Weininger, *Sex and Character* (1903), trans. Ladis-

	laus Löb (Bloomington: Indiana University Press, 2005)
SLBR	Nicholas Griffin, *The Selected Letters of Bertrand Russell*, vol. 1: *The Private Years, 1884–1914* (London: Penguin, 1992)
TLP	Ludwig Wittgenstein, *Tractatus Logico-Philosophicus*, 2nd ed., trans. D. F. Pears and B. F. McGuinness (London: Routledge, 1971)
TS	Typescript from Wittgenstein's *Nachlass*, Bergen Nachlass Edition, http://www.wittgensteinsource.org/
WFL	*Wittgenstein's Family Letters*, ed. Brian McGuinness, trans. Peter Winslow (London: Bloomsbury, 2019)
WIC	*Wittgenstein in Cambridge: Letters and Documents, 1911–1951*, ed. Brian McGuinness (Oxford: Blackwell, 2008)
YL	Brian McGuinness, *Wittgenstein: A Life. Young Ludwig (1889–1921)* (London: Duckworth, 1988)

Unattributed translations are my own.

Chapter 1. "A New Way of Philosophizing"

1. LW, diary entry, 7 February 1931, MT, 40.

2. "Ludwig Josef Johann Wittgenstein," Trinity College Chapel, http://trinitycollegechapel.com/about/memorials/brasses/wittgenstein/ (accessed 28 January 2025; translation altered).

3. LW, TLP, 3; LW, PI §109.

4. LW, diary entry, 8 February 1931, MT, 41; Heinrich Hertz, *The Principles of Mechanics* (1899), trans. D. Jones and J. Walley (New York: Dover, 1956), 8; Minutes of the Moral Sciences Club, 23 February 1939, in LW, *Public and Private Occasions*, ed. James C. Klagge and Alfred Nordmann (Oxford: Rowman & Littlefield, 2003), 379.

5. G. H. von Wright, "Intellectual Autobiography," in *The Philosophy of Georg Henrik von Wright*, ed. P. A. Schilpp and L. E. Hahn (La Salle, IL: Open Court, 1989), 42.

6. Hermine Wittgenstein, FE, 154.

7. *The Economist*, 25 January 1913, 175; *Times*, 22 January 1913, 9; *Die Fackel*, no. 65 (1901), 16, and no. 66 (1901), 27.

8. E. Fred Flindell, "Paul Wittgenstein, Patron and Pianist," *Music Review* 32, no. 2 (1971): 117.

9. *Times*, 2 May 1951, 8.

10. Drury, "Some Notes," in POW, 761; LW, 8 December 1914, in MS 102; Leo Tolstoy, *The Gospel in Brief*, trans. Dustin Condren (New York: Harper Perennial, 2011), xxi; LW, diary entry, 15 February 1937, MT, 80; Mathias Iven, *Ludwig sagt . . . : Die Aufzeichnungen der Hermine Wittgenstein* (Berlin: H-E Verlag, 2015), 99; G. E. M. Anscombe, *Der Monat*, no. 43 (1952): 87.

11. G. H. von Wright, "A Biographical Sketch," in Norman Malcolm, LWAM, 18; LW, 4 May 1916, in MS 103.

12. LW, diary entry, 11 January 1932, MT, 66; LW, diary entry, 2 March 1931, MT, 44.

13. *Die Neue Freie Presse*, 21 January 1913, 10.

Chapter 2. At Home with the Wittgensteins

1. Maurice Drury, "Conversations with Wittgenstein," in POW, 808. Quotations from this work reprinted by permission of the Philosophical Society of Finland and the Executor of the estate of M. O'C. Drury.

2. Erna Otten, letter to the *New York Times*, 24 April 2009; Brian McGuinness, "The Brothers Wittgenstein," in Irene Suchy, Allan Janik, and George A. Predota, eds., *Empty Sleeve: Der Musiker und Mäzen Paul Wittgenstein* (Innsbruck: Studienverlag, 2006), 57; Drury, "Conversations with Wittgenstein," in POW, 788; Paul Engelmann, LFLW, 90; Fania Pascal, "Wittgenstein: A Personal Memoir," in POW, 508.

3. WFL, 12, 17, 31.

4. Brian McGuinness, "Wittgenstein and Biography," in Oskari Kuusela and Marie McGinn, eds., *The Oxford Handbook of Wittgenstein* (Oxford: Oxford University Press, 2011), 16; Hermine Wittgenstein, FE, 130, 136.

5. Hermine Wittgenstein, FE, 142.

6. LW to Russell, 16 August 1912, in WIC, 34; David Pinsent, DP, 67.

7. Martin Alber, ed., *Wittgenstein und die Musik. Ludwig Wittgenstein—Rudolf Koder: Briefwechsel* (Innsbruck-Vienna: Haymon, 2014), 141.

8. Drury, "Conversations with Wittgenstein," in POW, 788; Eduard Hanslick, *Aus Meinem Leben* (1894) (Berlin: Holzinger, 2013), 330; E. Fred Flindell, "Paul Wittgenstein, Patron and Pianist," *Music Review* 32, no. 2 (1971): 120.

9. Leonard Kastle, in *Paul Wittgenstein: All in One Hand*, dir. Michael Beyer (Bernhard Fleischer Moving Images, 2009), at 43:40.

10. Hermine Wittgenstein, FE, 100.

11. *Die Neue Freie Presse*, 21 January 1913, 10.

12. Brian McGuinness, YL, 3.

13. Nicole Immler, *Das Familiengedächtnis Der Wittgensteins* (Bielefeld: Transkript Verlag, 2011), 220.

14. Hermine Wittgenstein, FE, 71; Theodore Redpath, "A Student's Memoir," in POW, 565; Norman Malcolm, LWAM, 24; Stephen Portman in *All in One Hand*, 41:10; Paul to LW, 17 November 1920, in WFL, 79; Ursula Prokop, *Margaret Stonborough-Wittgenstein: Bauherrin, Intellektuelle, Mäzenin* (Vienna: Bohlau, 2003), plate 14 after p. 152.

15. Hermine Wittgenstein, FE, 66–67; Ilse Somavilla, FE, 487; Allan Janik and Stephen Toulmin, *Wittgenstein's Vienna* (New York: Simon & Schuster, 1973), 171–72.

16. Georg Gaugusch, "Die Familien Wittgenstein und Salzer und ihr genealogisches Umfeld," *Adler—Zeitschrift für Genealogie und Heraldik* 21, no. 4 (2001): 123; A. F. Pribram, *Urkunden und Akten zur Geschichte der Juden in Wien*, vol. 2 (Vienna: Braumüller, 1918), 542. I am grateful to Elana Shapira, Irma Wulz, and Georg Gaugusch for help with this topic.

17. Brigitte Zwiauer, letter to the Reichstelle für Sippenforschung, 29 September 1938, Wiener Stadt-und Landesarchiv, https://crt-ii.org/_awards/_denials/_apdfs/Wittgenstein_Paul_den.pdf, 13 fn43 (accessed 28 January 2025).

18. Brigitte Hamann, *Hitler's Vienna* (London: Tauris, 2010), 335.

19. Hermine to LW, 1939, in WFL, 226; Peter Eigner, *Die Wittgensteins: Geschichte einer Unglaublich Reichen Familie* (Vienna: Molden, 2023), 207, 213; Kirk Ditzler, "Tradition ist 'Schlamperei': Gustav Mahler and the Vienna Court Opera," *International Review of the Aesthetics and Sociology of Music* 29, no. 1 (June 1998): 17.

20. Hermine Wittgenstein, FE, 78.

21. Hermine Wittgenstein, FE, 59.

22. Hermine Wittgenstein, FE, 60, 63, 62.

23. Paul Kupelwieser, *Aus den Erinnerungen eines alten Österreichers* (Vienna: Gerold, 1918), 61.

24. See J. Bramann and J. Moran, "Karl Wittgenstein, Business Tycoon and Art Patron," *Austrian History Yearbook* 15 (January 1979): 106–24; "Wittgenstein, Karl," in *Österreichisches Biographisches Lexikon, 1815–1950*, vol. 16, ed. Jakob Warchalowski and Marianna Emilie Zycha (Vienna: Verlag der Österreichischen Akademie der Wissenschaften, 2020), 293–94; Eigner, *Die Wittgensteins*, 67–109.

25. Hermine Wittgenstein, FE, 92.

26. Karl Wittgenstein, *Politico-economic Writings* (1913), ed. J. C. Nyiri (Amsterdam: Benjamins, 1984), 218 (translation amended), 59, 47.

27. LW, *Politico-Economic Writings*, 199, 68; Hermine Wittgenstein, FE, 99–100.

28. Prokop, *Margaret Stonborough-Wittgenstein*, 14; Hermine Wittgenstein, FE, 158; Alice Ambrose, "Ludwig Wittgenstein: A Portrait," in POW, 552; Wolfe Mays, "Recollections of Wittgenstein," in POW, 688.

29. Ambrose, "Ludwig Wittgenstein," in POW, 552; Rush Rhees to Alfred Kastil, 5 November 1933, quoted in James Klagge, "The Wittgenstein Lectures, Revisited," *Nordic Wittgenstein Review* 8, nos. 1–2 (2019): 37; Arthur Gibson and Niamh O'Mahony, eds., *Ludwig Wittgenstein: Dictating Philosophy To Francis Skinner* (Cham: Springer, 2020), 110.

30. Hermine Wittgenstein, FE, 147–48.

31. See Margaret Paul, *Frank Ramsey (1903–1930): A Sister's*

Memoir (Huntingdon: Smith-Gordon, 2012), 164; Hermine Wittgenstein, FE, 138, 141, 64–65.

32. Russell to Morrell, 7 March 1912, Bertrand Russell Archives, McMaster University, http://bracers.mcmaster.ca/17474 (accessed 28 January 2025); Maurice Drury, in "Ludwig Wittgenstein: A Symposium," POW, 1046.

33. Hermine Wittgenstein, FE, 489n31; radio interview with Paul Wittgenstein, WQXR, 20 May 1959, https://www.wnyc.org/story/paul-wittgenstein/ (accessed 28 January 2025), at 25:14.

34. Stefan Zweig, *Die Welt von Gestern* (1942) (Frankfurt: Fischer Verlag, 1970), 26–27.

35. *Grazer Volksblatt*, 4 May 1904, 4; Dr. Magnus Hirschfeld, *Jahrbuch für sexuelle Zwischenstufen*, vol. 6 (Leipzig, 1904), 724.

36. See Alexander Waugh, *The House of Wittgenstein* (New York: Doubleday, 2008), 121–23.

37. William M. Johnson, *The Austrian Mind: An Intellectual and Social History, 1848–1938* (Berkeley: University of California Press, 1983), 174; *Diskussionen des Wiener psychoanalytischen Vereins. Über den Selbstmord* (Wiesbaden: J. F. Bergmann, 1910), 16.

38. Hanslick, *Aus Meinem Leben*, 299.

39. Brigitte Hamann, *Rudolf: Crown Prince and Rebel*, trans. E. Borchardt (New York: Peter Lang, 2017), 365, 379, 378.

40. Hamann, *Rudolf*, 334.

41. LW, 11 February 1915, in MS 102.

Chapter 3. The Teacher Who Taught Himself

1. John Cater and Ian Lemco, "Wittgenstein's Combustion Chamber," *Notes & Records of the Royal Society* 63 (2009): 97; Russell to Morrell, 1 June 1912, in SLBR, 432.

2. LW to Hermine, 20 October 1908, in WFL, 46; Norbert Rosner, "My Memories of Herr Wittgenstein," in POW, 391; Ilse Somavilla, ed., *Begegnungen mit Wittgenstein: Ludwig Hänsels Tagebücher 1918/1919 und 1921/1922* (Innsbruck-Vienna: Haymon, 2012), 51 (as translated by James Klagge, private communication).

3. Brigitte Hamann, *Rudolf: Crown Prince and Rebel*, trans. E. Borchardt (New York: Peter Lang, 2017), 348, 390.

4. Hermine Wittgenstein, FE, 152; P. D. M. Spelt and Brian McGuinness, "Marginalia in Wittgenstein's Copy of Lamb's *Hydrodynamics*," in *From the Tractatus to the Tractatus and Other Essays*, ed. G. Oliveri (New York: Peter Lang, 2001), 131.

5. Brian McGuinness, YL, 52 (translation altered).

6. "Iconoclasm in German Philosophy," *Westminster Review* 59, no. 116 (1853): 212; Arthur Schopenhauer, *The World as Will and Representation*, trans. E. J. F. Payne (New York: Dover, 1969), index; German speakers and Schopenhauer: "What is the point? Didn't Schopenhauer say it all already?" This is what my German-born great-aunt Marie Sackin said in 1974 when I told her that I planned to study philosophy at university.

7. Schopenhauer, *World as Will*, 1:257, 260; G. E. M. Anscombe, *An Introduction to Wittgenstein's Tractatus* (London: Hutchinson, 1971), 11–12.

8. Arthur Schopenhauer, *The World as Will and Idea*, trans. R. B. Haldane and J. Kemp (London: Kegan Paul, 1909), 1; Arthur Schopenhauer, *Parerga and Paralipomena*, trans. E. J. F. Payne (Oxford: Oxford University Press, 1974), 2:291; Schopenhauer, *World as Will*, 1:196, 312.

9. Schopenhauer, *World as Will*, 1:185; Schopenhauer, *World as Will*, 2:605.

10. LW, NB, 79.

11. Ursula Prokop, *Margaret Stonborough-Wittgenstein: Bauherrin, Intellektuelle, Mäzenin* (Vienna: Bohlau, 2003), 97; Arthur Schopenhauer, *On the Fourfold Root of the Principle of Sufficient Reason and Other Writings* (Cambridge: Cambridge University Press, 2012), 325.

12. Emil du Bois-Reymond, "The Limits of Our Knowledge of Nature," *Popular Science Monthly* 5 (May 1874): 17; Ludwig Büchner, *Kraft und Stoff* (1855), 10th ed. (Leipzig: Theodor Thomas, 1869), 268.

13. *Neue Freie Presse*, 27 October 1903, 5–6.

14. Ludwig Boltzmann, *Theoretical Physics and Philosophical Problems*, ed. Brian McGuinness (Dordrecht: D. Reidel, 1974), 185, 192.

15. Boltzmann, *Theoretical Physics*, 163, 167; *Ludwig Boltzmann: Principien der Naturfilosofi*, ed. Ilse M. Fasol-Boltzmann (Berlin:

Springer-Verlag, 1990), 71–72 (translation corrected); Ernst Mach, *Popular Scientific Lectures*, trans. T. J. McCormack (Chicago: Open Court, 1898), 308 (emphasis corrected); Boltzmann, *Theoretical Physics*, 167.

16. Ludwig Boltzmann, "On Aeronautics," (as translated in Susan Sterrett, *Wittgenstein Flies a Kite* [New York: Pi, 2006], 263).

17. LW, C&V, 16; David Abrahamsen, *The Mind and Death of a Genius* (New York: Columbia University Press, 1946), 207.

18. Stefan Zweig, *Die Welt von Gestern* (1942) (Frankfurt: Fischer Verlag, 1970), 127; *Die Fackel*, no. 1 (1899), 2 (as translated by E. F. Timms in *Karl Kraus: Apocalyptic Satirist* [New Haven: Yale University Press, 1986], 41); *Die Fackel*, no. 443 (1916), 6.

19. *Die Fackel*, nos. 376–77 (1913), 21; *Die Fackel*, no. 300 (1910), 27.

20. *Die Fackel*, nos. 557–60 (1921), 63.

21. *Die Fackel*, nos. 261–62 (1908), 1 (as translated by Timms in *Karl Kraus*, 149); *Die Fackel*, no. 241 (1908), 14–15.

22. Robert Wistrich, *The Jews of Vienna in the Age of Franz Joseph* (Oxford: Oxford University Press, 1990), 515; Lettice Ramsey to Friedrich Hayek, 1953, in Nicole Immler, *Das Familiengedächtnis Der Wittgensteins* (Bielefeld: Transkript Verlag, 2011), 159; LW, diary entry, MT, 93; LW, C&V, 76.

23. Paul Engelmann, LFLW, 126, 122–23, 123; *Die Fackel*, nos. 360–62 (1912), 16; LW, PO, 44; LW, PI §119.

24. LW, TLP 6.421; Paul Engelmann, LFLW, 125–26; draft letter to Adele Jolles, circa 1930, in Brian McGuinness, YL, 59; LW to Donald Coxeter, 13 January 1934, in WIC, 220; LW to W. H. Watson, 13 June 1932, in WIC, 201.

25. LW, OLT, 136; Otto Weininger, S&C, 299.

26. Otto Weininger, S&C, 376, iv–x.

27. Sigmund Freud, *Little Hans*, in *The "Wolfman" and Other Cases*, trans. Louise Adey Huish (New York: Penguin, 2003), 81; Abrahamsen, *The Mind and Death*, 55; Stefan Zweig, "Vorbeigehen an einem unauffälligen Menschen—Otto Weininger" (1926), in *Zeiten und Schicksale* (Frankfurt: Fischer, 1990), 298–302; Elias Canetti, *The Torch in My Ear* (London: Andre Deutsch, 1989), 77.

28. Michael Robinson, *Studies in Strindberg* (London: Ubiquity, 2013), 137; Chandak Sengoopta, *Otto Weininger: Sex, Science, and Self in Imperial Vienna* (Chicago: University of Chicago Press, 2000), 140.

29. Hermine to LW, 18 November 1916, in WFL, 15.

30. LW to Moore, 23 August 1931, in WIC, 193.

31. Drury, "Some Notes," in POW, 770–71.

32. LW, OLT, 7, 31; "Remembering My Cousin, Ludwig Wittgenstein," in POW, 131; Joseph Wechsberg, "His Hand Touched Our Hearts," *Coronet*, June 1959, 28.

33. Otto Weininger, S&C, 139, 152, 286; WIC, 63; Gretl on reformers: Karl Menger, "Reminiscences of the Wittgenstein Family," in POW, 118; LW on Gretl: Gabriel Citron, "Wittgenstein's Philosophical Conversations with Rush Rhees (1939–50)," *Mind* 124, no. 493 (January 2015): 12.

34. Hermann Broch, *Philosophische Schriften 1* (Berlin: Suhrkamp, 1986), 248; Otto Weininger, S&C, 312, 302.

35. Otto Weininger, S&C, 3, 307, 306, 274, 293, 275.

36. Otto Weininger, S&C 293, 278, 288, 273; Geoffrey Field, *Evangelist of Race: The Germanic Vision of Houston Stewart Chamberlain* (New York: Columbia University Press, 1981), 116.

37. Otto Weininger, S&C, 283, 284.

38. LW, OLT, 137, 135.

39. LW, TS 219, 8; LW, TLP 6.372; LW, "A Lecture on Ethics," in LW, PO, 37; O. K. Bouwsma, *Wittgenstein: Conversations, 1949–51*, ed. J. L. Craft and Ronald E. Hustwit (Indianapolis: Hackett, 1986), 28.

40. LW, OLT, 68; *Die Fackel*, no. 145 (1903); Weininger's zoological typology: LW, OLT, 103–9; Drury, "Conversations with Wittgenstein," in POW, 789.

41. Mathias Iven, *Ludwig sagt . . . : Die Aufzeichnungen der Hermine Wittgenstein* (Berlin: HE Verlag, 2015), 127.

42. Otto Weininger, S&C, 286; Hillary Hope Herzog, *Vienna Is Different: Jewish Writers in Austria from the Fin-de-Siècle to the Present* (New York: Berghahn Books, 2011), 55; LW, C&V, 16.

43. LW, C&V, 17; Otto Friedländer, *Letzter Glanz der Märchenstadt* (Vienna: Ring-Verlag, 1948), 33. See also *Arbeiter-Zeitung*,

13 April 1930, 9; Arthur Schnitzler, *The Road to the Open* (Evanston: Northwestern University Press, 1991), 104.

44. LW, C&V, 23, 17, 8, 17, 43, 3, 17; LW, diary entry, MT, 108; LW, C&V, 19, 18.

45. Kirk Willis, "'This Place Is Hell': Bertrand Russell at Harvard, 1914," *New England Quarterly* 62, no 1. (March 1989): 14–15; Russell, "On Keeping a Wide Horizon," *Russell: The Journal of Bertrand Russell Studies*, nos. 33–34 (Spring–Summer 1979): 10. (This passage was apparently removed by the editors of *Reader's Digest*.)

46. LW, C&V, 17, 42.

47. Neville Cardus, *Autobiography* (London: Readers Union, 1949), 48.

48. Rush Rhees, notes to Hermine Wittgenstein's "My Brother Ludwig," in POW, 121n1.

49. Wolfe Mays, "Wittgenstein in Manchester," in POW, 145, 141, 145; LW to Hermine, 20 October 1908, in WFL, 6.

50. Patent GB-1910-27087; see Michael Potter, *Wittgenstein's Notes on Logic* (Oxford: Oxford University Press, 2009), 9–10; and Ian Lemco, "Wittgenstein's Aeronautical Investigation," *Notes and Records of the Royal Society*, January 22, 2007, 39–51.

51. Alfred North Whitehead and Bertrand Russell, *Principia Mathematica*, 2nd ed. (Cambridge: Cambridge University Press, 1927), 2:83; Bertrand Russell, *The Principles of Mathematics*, 2nd ed. (London: Allen & Unwin, 1937), 42.

52. Russell, *Principles of Mathematics*, 502.

53. Bertrand Russell, *My Philosophical Development* (London: Allen & Unwin, 1959), 75; Bertrand Russell, *Logic and Knowledge* (London: Allen & Unwin, 1956), 261; Frege to Russell, 22 June 1902, in Gottlob Frege, *Philosophical and Mathematical Correspondence* (Oxford: Blackwell, 1980), 132.

54. Russell, *Principles of Mathematics*, 523, 528.

55. Russell to Morrell, 21 March 1912, in Russell, CPBR, xxviii.

Chapter 4. The Next Big Step

1. Russell, CPBR, xxv.
2. Russell, CPBR, xxvi.

3. David Pinsent, DP, 6; Ludwig Anzengruber, *Die Kreuzelschreiber* (1872), act III, scene 1; Stefan Zweig, *Die Welt von Gestern* (1942) (Frankfurt: Fischer Verlag, 1970), 456; Sigmund Freud, *Reflections on War and Death*, trans. A. A. Brill and Alfred B. Kuttner (New York: Moffat, Yard, 1918), 63; LW, "A Lecture on Ethics," in PO, 42; Norman Malcolm, LWAM , 58.

4. Russell to Morrell, 5 March 1912, in Brian McGuinness, YL, 117; Russell to Morrell, 10 March 1912, in Russell, CPBR, xxvii; Russell to Morrell, 18 March 1912, in SLBR, 418–19.

5. Russell to Morrell, 16 March 1912, in Russell, CPBR, xxvii; Moore to F. A. Hayek, undated, in Ray Monk, DG, 63; F. R. Leavis, "Memories of Wittgenstein," in POW, 545.

6. David Pinsent, DP, 4–5.

7. David Pinsent, DP, 59.

8. David Pinsent, DP, 75; Russell to Morrell, 27 May 1912, in Brian McGuinness, YL, 104 (date corrected).

9. LW to Russell, summer 1912, in WIC, 23.

10. LW to Russell, 22 June 1912, in WIC, 30; Russell, *Introduction to Mathematical Philosophy* (London: Allen & Unwin, 1919), 169; LW, TLP 6.124; LW, TLP 6.121; LW to Russell, November or December 1913, in WIC, 58; W. E. Johnson, *Logic: Part 1* (Cambridge: Cambridge University Press, 1921), 105.

11. LW, "On Logic, and How Not to Do It," *Cambridge Review* 34 (1912–13) (LW, PO, 3); Wittgenstein credited Russell: LW, TLP 4.0031.

12. Russell, *History of Western Philosophy* (1946) (London: Allen & Unwin, 1961), 785.

13. Russell to Gilbert Murray, 7 August 1911, in Russell, CPBR, xlii; Russell to Morrell, 13 December 1911, in SLBR, 404; Bertrand Russell, *The Problems of Philosophy* (1912) (Oxford: Oxford University Press, 1959), 1.

14. Russell to Morrell, 18 March 1912, in SLBR, 419; LW to Russell, February 1914, in WIC, 67 (translation altered). This letter is in German: Wittgenstein wrote of the value of a "wissenschaftlichen" work. Although this word is often translated as "scientific,"

it is broader than the English term, and Wittgenstein at this stage referred to his own philosophical work as "wissenschaftlich."

15. Russell, *Problems of Philosophy*, 94; Plato: *Republic*, book VI, 500c.

16. Russell, "The Philosophy of Logical Atomism" (1918), in *Logic and Knowledge*, ed. Robert C. Marsh (London: Allen & Unwin, 1956), 281; Russell, "Logical Positivism" (1950), in Russsell, *Logic and Knowledge*, 371.

17. Russell, *Problems of Philosophy*, 87; "Minutes of the Moral Sciences Club, 29.11.1912," in WIC, 35.

18. LW, B&BB, 18.

19. Russell, "On Scientific Method in Philosophy" (1914), in *Mysticism and Logic* (London: Allen & Unwin, 1917), 103.

20. Russell to Morrell, 18 March 1912, in SLBR, 419; Russell to Morrell, 1 June 1912, in SLBR, 432.

21. David Pinsent, DP, 67.

22. Desmond Lee, "Wittgenstein 1929–1931," in POW, 482.

23. LW, diary entry, MT, 45; LW, TLP 6.421; LW, TLP 6.41.

24. Rush Rhees, "Postscript," in POW, 850; Lee, "Wittgenstein, 1929–1931," in POW, 482; Norman Malcolm, in LWAM, 52–53; G. H. von Wright, "Intellectual Autobiography," in *The Philosophy of Georg Henrik von Wright*, ed. P. A. Schilpp and L. E. Hahn (La Salle, IL: Open Court, 1989), 14.

25. Russell to Morrell, 9 November 1912, in Russell, CPBR, xxxiii.

26. Russell to Morrell, 31 October 1912, in Russell, CPBR, xvii.

27. Russell to Morrell, 2 May 1912, in Russell, CPBR, xxix; Brian McGuinness, YL, 119, 151.

28. LW to Russell, 21 January 1913, in WIC, 39.

29. David Pinsent, DP, 86; David Pinsent, DP, 44; Rhees, "Postscript," in POW, 849; Peter Conradi, *Iris Murdoch: A Life* (New York: Harper Collins, 2002), 266.

30. Russell to Morrell, 23 April 1913, in Russell, CPBR, xxxiv; Ray Monk, DG, 434; Russell to Morrell, in Russell, CPBR, xxxiv.

31. Wittgenstein's example: LW, "Notes on Logic," in NB, 103;

attempts to reconstruct Wittgenstein's objection: see, e.g., James R. Connelly, *Wittgenstein's Critique of Russell's Multiple Relation Theory of Judgement* (London: Anthem, 2021).

32. LW to Russell, 22 July 1913, in WIC, 42.

33. LW to Russell, 5 September 1913, in WIC, 45; David Pinsent, DP, 67, 56, 79.

34. David Pinsent, DP, 80.

35. David Pinsent, DP, 85.

36. Russell to Morrell, 4 October 1913, in Russell, CPBR, xxxvi.

37. David Pinsent, DP, 88; Russell to Morrell, 2 October 1913, in Russell, CPBR, xxxvi.

38. *Ottoline: The Early Memoirs of Lady Ottoline Morrell*, ed. R. Gathorne-Hardy (London: Faber, 1963), 273; Bertrand Russell, *Portraits from Memory* (London: Allen & Unwin, 1956), 108; Russell, "Ludwig Wittgenstein," *Mind* 60, no. 239 (July 1951): 298.

39. LW to Russell, 29 October 1913, in WIC, 49; LW to Russell, November 1913, in WIC, 50.

40. LW to Russell, November or December 1913, in WIC, 58–59; LW to Russell, 15 December 1913, in WIC, 61.

41. E. Fred Flindell, "Paul Wittgenstein, Patron and Pianist," *Music Review* 32, no. 2 (1971): 112.

42. LW to Russell, Christmas 1913, in WIC, 63.

43. LW to Russell, 3 March 1914, in WIC, 71.

44. LW to Russell, 19 August 1919, in WIC, 98; LW, NB, 108 (spelling altered).

45. LW, TLP 6.522; LW, TLP 7 (both in Ramsey-Ogden translation).

46. LW, 25 February 1949, in MS 138; LW to Malcolm, 20 September 1945, in WIC, 385; LW to Engelmann, 9 April 1917, in LFLW, 7.

47. LW to Moore, 7 May 1914, in WIC, 73.

48. David Pinsent, DP, 89.

49. Russell to Morrell, 12 November 1914, in Russell, CPBR, xxxviii; Békássy to Olivier, May 1915, in Ferenc Békássy, *The Alien in the Chapel*, ed. George Gömöri and Mari Gömöri (Bloxham: Skyscraper, 2016), 185.

50. Hermine Wittgenstein, FE, 154; Russell to Morrell, 29 May 1912 (quoted with permission from the Bertrand Russell Archives, McMaster University); Brian McGuinness, YL, 204; LW, 15 September 1914, in MS 101; LW, 4 May 1916, in MS 103.

51. Russell, *Autobiography* (London: Routledge, 2010), 251.

52. Russell, *Introduction to Mathematical Philosophy* (London: Allen & Unwin, 1919), 205n1.

53. LW, 29 July 1916, in MS 103.

54. LW, 1929, in MS 106, 4.

55. LW, 26 July 1916, in MS 103; LW to Russell, 23 October 1921, in WIC, 126.

56. LW, 12 September 1914, in MS 101 (as translated in Brian McGuinness, YL, 221; date amended).

57. LW, 21 December 1914, in MS 102.

58. LW to Russell, 6 August 1920, in WIC, 122; David Pinsent, DP, 109.

59. LW, NB, 79 (translation altered); LW, NB, 74–75.

60. LW, NB, 74.

61. LW, TLP 4.11.

62. LW, NB, 8; LW, TLP 4.021.

63. LW, TLP, preface.

64. LW, TLP 5.634.

65. Russell, introduction to LW, TLP, xxi.

66. LW, C&V, 10; LW, PI, x; G. E. M. Anscombe, *An Introduction to Wittgenstein's Tractatus* (London: Hutchinson, 1971), 78; Euan Hill, "Whatever Happened to Wisdom?" *Think* 17, no. 48 (Spring 2018): 121. See also James C. Klagge, *Tractatus in Context* (London: Routledge, 2022), 314.

67. LW, TLP, preface; LW to Russell, 13 March 1919, in WIC, 89.

68. LW, TLP, preface; LW to Hermine, 25 June 1919, in WFL, 60–61.

Chapter 5. Work on Oneself

1. Russell to Morrell, 20 December 1919, in WIC, 112.

2. Paul Engelmann, LFLW, 78; Mays, "Wittgenstein in Manchester," in POW, 141.

3. Russell to Morrell, 16 October 1911, in SLBR, 396; Engelmann to von Hayek, 8 March 1953, quoted with permission from the von Wright and Wittgenstein Archives, University of Helsinki; Engelmann to von Hayek (Engelmann's emphasis).

4. LW to Ficker, 19 July 1914, in LW, *Briefe an Ludwig von Ficker* (Salzburg: Müller Verlag, 1969), 12.

5. LW to Engelmann, 19 February 1920, in LFLW, 29; LW to Ficker, 22 November 1919, in LW, *Briefe an von Ficker*, 37; LW to Engelmann, 30 May 1920, in LFLW, 33; LW to Engelmann, 21 June 1920, in LFLW, 33.

6. LW to Engelmann, 2 January 1921, in LFLW, 41.

7. Russell to Colette O'Niel, 12 December 1919, in Nicholas Griffin, ed., *The Selected Letters of Bertrand Russell: The Public Years, 1914–1970* (London: Routledge, 2001), 197; Russell to Morrell, 20 December 1919, in WIC, 112.

8. LW, TLP, preface; LW to Russell, 13 March 1919, in WIC, 89.

9. LW to Russell, 6 May 1920, in WIC, 120.

10. Ronald W. Clark, *The Life of Bertrand Russell* (New York: Knopf, 1976), 378.

11. LW to Engelmann, 20 August 1920, in LFLW, 37.

12. Karl Kodek, *Der Monat*, no. 43 (1952): 98; LW to Russell, 20 September 1920, in WIC, 123.

13. LW to Ludwig Hänsel, 20 September 1919, in *Ludwig Hänsel—Ludwig Wittgenstein: Eine Freundschaft*, ed. Ilse Somavilla, Anton Unterkircher, and Christian Paul Berger (Innsbruck: Haymon, 1994), 19; Hermine to LW, 23 November 1920, in WFL, 85.

14. LW to Russell, 23 October 1921, in WIC, 126.

15. LW to Russell, 28 November 1921, in WIC, 128; Rudolf Carnap, "Intellectual Autobiography," in *The Philosophy of Rudolf Carnap*, ed. P. A. Schilpp (La Salle: Open Court, 1963), 26.

16. Ogden to Russell, 5 November 1921, in LW, *Letters to C. K. Ogden* (Oxford: Blackwell, 1973), 3.

17. For an overview of Ramsey's work, see my "The Man Who Thought Too Fast," *New Yorker*, 27 April 2020; LW, PI, preface.

18. LW to Russell, November or December 1922, in WIC, 136; Norbert Rosner, "My Memories of Herr Wittgenstein," in POW, 391.

19. Ramsey to Ogden, September 1923, in WIC, 140.

20. Ramsey to Agnes Ramsey, 20 September 1923, in WIC, 139.

21. Ramsey to LW, 11 November 1923, in WIC, 143; Frank Ramsey, "Philosophy," in *Frank Ramsey: Philosophical Papers*, ed. D. H. Mellor (Cambridge: Cambridge University Press, 1990), 1.

22. Ramsey to LW, 11 November 1923, in WIC, 143; Margaret Paul, "Wittgenstein and Ramsey," in POW, 415–16.

23. Moritz Schlick, "The Present Task of Philosophy" (1911), in *Philosophical Papers*, vol. 1, ed. Henk L. Mulder and Barbara F. B. van de Velde-Schlick (Dordrecht: D. Reidel, 1979), 104; Moritz Schlick, *General Theory of Knowledge* (La Salle: Open Court, 1985), v.

24. Schlick to Hans Reichenbach, 5 August 1924, in Cheryl Misak, *Frank Ramsey* (Oxford: Oxford University Press, 2022), 174; Schlick to LW, 25 December 1924, in LFLW, 146; Schlick to Einstein, 14 July 1927, in Mathias Iven, "Er 'ist eine Künstlernatur von hinreissender Genialität,'" *Wittgenstein-Studien* 6, no. 1 (2015): 97.

25. Ramsey to Agnes Ramsey, 30 March 1924, in WIC, 148; Ramsey to Keynes, April 1924, in POW, 415.

26. LW to Keynes, 4 July 1924, in WIC, 153.

27. Keynes to Lopokova, 4 May 1924, in *Lydia & Maynard*, ed. Polly Hill and Richard Keynes (New York: Scribners, 1989), 183; Robert Skidelsky, *John Maynard Keynes, 1883–1946* (London: Penguin, 2005), 357; Ramsey to Lettice Baker, n.d., in Misak, *Frank Ramsey*, 241; LW, diary entry, 27 April 1930, in MT, 19.

28. LW to Keynes, 18 October 1925, in WIC, 157; Luise Hausmann and Eugene C. Hargrove, "Wittgenstein in Austria as an Elementary-School Teacher," in POW, 393.

29. LW to Rudolf Koder, Autumn 1926, in *Wittgenstein und Die Musik*, ed. Martin Alber (Innsbruck: Haymon, 2014), 16.

30. Drury, "Conversations with Wittgenstein," in POW, 784; Lee, "Wittgenstein, 1929–1931," in POW, 478.

31. Engelmann to von Hayek, n.d., in Paul Wijdeveld, *Ludwig Wittgenstein: Architect* (Amsterdam: Pepin, 1993), 53.

32. Russell to Morrell, 5 September 1912, in Russell, CPBR, xxx; David Pinsent, DP, 8; Katharine Tait, *My Father Bertrand Russell* (Bristol: Thoemmes, 1996), 116; David Pinsent, DP, 56.

33. Adolf Loos, *Ornament and Crime: Selected Essays* (Riverside: Ariadne, 1998), 167; Paul Engelmann, LFLW, 17.

34. Wijdeveld, *Ludwig Wittgenstein: Architect*, 114; Josef Rothhaupt and Aidan Seery, "*Ludwig Wittgenstein war ein 'Stern' in meinem Leben*—Interview mit Marguerite de Chambrier," in *Wittgenstein-Jahrbuch 2000* (Frankfurt: Peter Lang, 2001), 127; Hermine Wittgenstein, FE, 163 (as translated by Rush Rhees in POW, 125).

35. Hermine Wittgenstein, FE, 164 (as translated by Rush Rhees in POW, 125–26).

36. Hermine to Ludwig, 22 November 1929, WFL, 161.

37. Otto Neurath, *Empiricism & Sociology* (Dordrecht: D. Reidel, 1973), 317, 307, 306.

38. Moritz Schlick, "The Turning-Point in Philosophy" (1930), *Philosophical Papers*, vol. 2, ed. Henk L. Mulder and Barbara F. B. van de Velde-Schlick (Dordrecht: D. Reidel, 1979), 156.

39. Paul Engelmann, LFLW, 97.

40. LW, TLP 4.003.

41. Carnap, "Intellectual Autobiography," 24; Herbert Feigl, *Inquiries and Provocations: Selected Writings, 1929–1974*, ed. R. S. Cohen (Dordrecht: D. Reidel, 1981), 8.

42. Carnap, "Intellectual Autobiography," 26–27.

43. Feigl, *Inquiries and Provocations*, 63; LW, diary entry, 28 April 1930, in MT, 19.

44. Carnap, "Intellectual Autobiography," 26.

45. LW, *Wittgenstein's Lectures on the Foundations of Mathematics, Cambridge, 1939*, ed. Cora Diamond (Chicago: University of Chicago Press, 1975), 237; Feigl, *Inquiries and Provocations*, 64.

46. Knut Tranøy, "Wittgenstein in Cambridge, 1949–51: Some Personal Recollections," in POW, 1022.

47. LW, 14 October 1931, in C&V, 24; LW to Keynes, 1928, in WIC, 163; Rothhaupt and Seery, "Interview mit Marguerite," 134.

48. Hermine Wittgenstein, FE, 159 (as translated by Rush Rhees in POW, 124); Anthony Kenny, "Aquinas and Wittgenstein," *Downside Review* 77, no. 249 (July 1959): 253.

49. LW, *Lectures and Conversations on Aesthetics, Psychology and Religious Belief*, ed. Cyril Barrett (Oxford: Blackwell, 1978), 1.

50. Skidelsky, *John Maynard Keynes*, 401.

Chapter 6. The Stream of Life

1. LW, *Last Writings on the Philosophy of Psychology*, vol. 1 (Oxford: Blackwell, 1982), 118; LW, PI §23.

2. LW, PI §116.

3. LW, PI §38; LW, *On Certainty*, ed. G. E. M. Anscombe and G. H. von Wright (Oxford: Blackwell, 1969), §341–42.

4. Ray Monk, DG, 261; LW, *Remarks on the Foundations of Mathematics*, 3rd ed. (Oxford: Blackwell, 1978), 399; Amartya Sen, "Sraffa, Wittgenstein, and Gramsci," *Journal of Economic Literature* 41 (December 2003): 1243.

5. Keynes to Lopokova, 25 February 1929, in Cheryl Misak, *Frank Ramsey* (Oxford: Oxford University Press, 2022), 347; LW, 15 February 1929, in MS 105.

6. G. E. Moore, "Wittgenstein's Lectures in 1930–33," in LW, PO, 48; Ramsey to Sebastian Sprott, 1929, in Misak, *Frank Ramsey*, 349, 359.

7. Ramsey to LW, Spring 1929, in WIC, 167.

8. Frank Ramsey, "Philosophy," in *Frank Ramsey: Philosophical Papers*, ed. D. H. Mellor (Cambridge: Cambridge University Press, 1990); LW, *Lectures and Conversations on Aesthetics, Psychology and Religious Belief*, ed. Cyril Barrett (Oxford: Blackwell, 1978), 2.

9. G. E. M. Anscombe, *From Plato to Wittgenstein: Essays by G. E. M. Anscombe*, ed. Mary Geach and Luke Gormally (Exeter: Imprint Academic, 2011), 177; LW, "A Lecture on Ethics," in PO, 41.

10. LW, PO, 44.

11. "Arthur MacIver's Diary: Cambridge (October 1929—March 1930)," ed. Brian McGuinness, *Wittgenstein-Studien* 7 (2016): 220; Lucia Morra, "Wittgenstein in Alethea Graham's Diary (1929–1930), and New Data on the Audience of His Lecture on Ethics and LT 1930 class," *Nordic Wittgenstein Review* 13 (2024), prepublication copy, 4.

12. Brian McGuinness, ed., *Ludwig Wittgenstein and the Vienna Circle* (Oxford: Blackwell, 1979), 68–69.

13. McGuinness, *Wittgenstein and the Vienna Circle*, 47; LW, *Wittgenstein's Lectures, Cambridge, 1930–32*, ed. Desmond Lee (Totowa: Rowman & Littlefield, 1980), 66; *The Philosophy of Rudolf Carnap*, ed. P. A. Schilpp (La Salle: Open Court, 1963), 44.

14. Ernst Mach, *The Science of Mechanics* (1883), ch. IV.4, trans. T. J. McCormack (Open Court, 1960), 587; "Discussions between Wittgenstein, Waddington, and Thouless," in LW, *Public and Private Occasions*, ed. James C. Klagge and Alfred Nordmann (Lanham: Rowman & Littlefield, 2003), 396.

15. D. A. T. Gasking and A. C. Jackson, "Ludwig Wittgenstein," in POW, 1039.

16. LW, diary entry, 25 April 1930, in MT, 16n7; LW, diary entry, 9 May 1930, in MT, 25; Gretl to Thomas Stonborough, Autumn 1929, in Ursula Prokop, *Margaret Stonborough-Wittgenstein: Bauherrin, Intellektuelle, Mäzenin* (Vienna: Bohlau, 2003), 193.

17. Gretl to LW, 18 February 1932, in Prokop, *Margaret Stonborough-Wittgenstein*, 209.

18. LW, diary entry, 28 January 1932, in MT, 68; LW to W. H. Watson, 19 August 1931, in WIC, 192.

19. LW, *Wittgenstein's Lectures, Cambridge 1930–32*, 1; LW, *Wittgenstein: Lectures, Cambridge, 1930–33: From the Notes of G. E. Moore*, ed. David G. Stern, Brian Rogers, and Gabriel Citron (Cambridge: Cambridge University Press, 2016), 5.

20. LW to Russell, January 1914, in WIC, 66; J. N. Findlay, *Wittgenstein: A Critique* (Routledge, 1984), 20; Michael Ignatieff, *Isaiah Berlin: A Life* (New York: Metropolitan Books, 1998), 94.

21. LW, 20 January 1930, in MS 107; LW, diary entry, 27 April 1930, in MT, 18–19.

22. Russell, "Critical Notice of *The Foundations of Mathematics and Other Logical Essays*," *Mind* 40, no. 160 (October 1931): 482; LW, 1 November 1931, in C&V, 24.

23. LW, 6-7 November 1930, in C&V, 8–9.

24. Drury, "Conversations with Wittgenstein," in POW, 788; LW, C&V, 4.

25. Raffaello Piccoli, *Italian Humanities: An Inaugural Lecture* (1929) (Cambridge: Cambridge University Press, 2014), 28–34. See also Lucia Morra, "Wittgenstein and Piccoli," *Wittgenstein-Studien* 11, no. 1 (2020): 1–29.

26. Sir James Jeans, *The Mysterious Universe* (Cambridge: Cambridge University Press, 1930), 3rd impression, cover; Drury, "Conversations with Wittgenstein," in POW, 793.

27. Drury, "Conversations with Wittgenstein," in POW, 788; R. Rhees, "Postscript," in POW, 861; LW, 7 January 1947, in C&V, 64.

28. R. B. Braithwaite, To the Editor of *Mind*, 27 May 1933, in LW, PO, 157.

29. Friedrich Stadler, *The Vienna Circle: Studies in the Origins, Development, and Influence of Logical Empiricism* (Vienna: Springer, 2001), 431–33; Paul Wittgenstein to Siegfried Rapp, 6 May 1950, in Alexander Waugh, *The House of Wittgenstein* (New York: Doubleday, 2008), 279.

30. M. K. Rowe, *J. L. Austin: Philosopher and D-Day Intelligence Officer* (Oxford: Oxford University Press, 2023), 145. See also Daniel W. Harris and Elmar Unnsteinsson, "Wittgenstein's Influence on Austin's Philosophy of Language," *British Journal for the History of Philosophy* 26, no. 2 (2018): 371–95.

31. LW, B&BB, 41, 47; private language: LW, PI §258–59.

32. Gilbert Ryle, *The Concept of Mind* (London: Hutchinson, 1949), 15–16, 13; J. J. C. Smart, quoted in *History of Philosophy in Australia and New Zealand*, ed. G. Oppy and N. N. Trakakis (Dordrecht: Springer Netherlands, 2004), 113.

33. LW, B&BB, 48, 17.

34. LW, PI §66–67.

35. LW, B&BB, 43.

36. LW, B&BB, 1, 6.

37. LW, B&BB, 17, 46, 52, 66, 67; Gabriella Bottini et al., "Feeling Touches in Someone Else's Hand," *Neuroreport* 13, no. 2 (2002): 249–52.

38. Nuno Venturinha, "Sraffa's Notes on Wittgenstein's *Blue Book*," *Nordic Wittgenstein Review* 1, no. 1 (2012): 184.

39. Plato, *Sophist*, 256b–268c; Aristotle, *Physics*, 186a24; Hobbes, *Leviathan*, ch. 46; Nietzsche, *Human, All Too Human*, trans. R. J. Hollingdale (Cambridge: Cambridge University Press, 1986), 306. (Wittgenstein echoed Nietzsche's remark: LW, *The Big Typescript: TS 213*, ed. and trans. C. Grant Luckhardt and Maximilian A. E. Aue [Oxford: Blackwell, 2005], 317.)

40. LW, *Big Typescript*, 309, 310 (LW, PI §123); LW, B&BB, 27, 28.

41. LW, 4 September 1937, in C&V, 32; LW, 21 December 1947, in C&V, 73; Norman Malcolm, LWAM, 60; G. H. von Wright, "Wittgenstein in Relation to His Times," in *Wittgenstein and His Times*, ed. Brian McGuinness (Oxford: Blackwell, 1982), 119.

42. Fania Pascal, "Wittgenstein: A Personal Memoir," in POW, 517, 516, 512; LW, diary entry, 16 October 1930, in MT, 35.

43. Gilbert Pattinson, quoted in Michael Nedo, "Ludwig Wittgenstein: A Chronology," in POW, 53–54.

44. Keynes to Ivan Maisky, 10 July 1935, in WIC, 246; Pascal, "Personal Memoir," in POW, 531–52; Drury, "Conversations with Wittgenstein," in POW, 815; Josef Rothhaupt and Aidan Seery, "*Ludwig Wittgenstein war ein 'Stern' in meinem Leben*—Interview mit Marguerite de Chambrier," in *Wittgenstein-Jahrbuch 2000* (Frankfurt: Peter Lang, 2001), 134.

45. Stadler, *Vienna Circle*, 898, 873, 876.

46. LW, diary entry, in MT, 76.

47. LW, PI §1. Passages quoted and described from this Norway manuscript (LW, MS 142) are substantially identical to the published PI.

48. LW, PI §124; Ludwig Boltzmann, *Theoretical Physics and Philosophical Problems*, ed. Brian McGuinness (D. Reidel, 1974), 193; LW, PI §118 (translation altered).

49. LW to Hänsel, 7 November 1936, in MT, 115.

50. LW, diary entry, 19 November 1936, in MT, 69; LW, diary entry, 23 November 1936, in MT, 71; Skinner to LW, 9 December 1936, in GBW.

51. Pascal, "A Personal Memoir," in POW, 526.

52. LW, diary entry, 24 February 1937, in MT, 93; LW, diary entry, 16 March 1937, in MT, 97.

53. LW, 22 September 1937, in MS 118; LW, 23 October 1937, in MS 119; LW, 16 November 1937, in MS 119; 21 November 1937, in MS 120.

The remark about laying with Francis is the only evidence that Wittgenstein ever had sex, apart from his hint that he had been with a woman in his youth. In her edition and translation of Wittgenstein's wartime notebooks (*Private Notebooks, 1914–16* [New York: Liveright, 2022]), Marjorie Perloff asserted that they contain "telling allusions to gay rendezvous" (199). The German text does not support this. She stated that Wittgenstein "records frequent trips to the baths . . . in town" (81), though in fact he merely recorded having bathed. When Wittgenstein wrote in January 1915 that "my moral standing is now much lower than it was at Easter" (121), Perloff comments that the "allusion is probably to some sexual affair" (81) but provides no grounds for this speculation.

In his *Wittgenstein* (Philadelphia: Lippincott, 1973, 47), W. W. Bartley III stated that Wittgenstein was promiscuous with "rough young men" in Vienna when he was training to be a teacher. Bartley did not give any source for this claim. See Ray Monk's discussion of Bartley's assertions: DG, 581–86.

54. LW, 11 September 1937, in MS 117; LW, 26 September 1937, in MS 119; LW, *Wittgenstein's Lectures on the Foundations of Mathematics, Cambridge, 1939*, ed. Cora Diamond (Chicago: University of Chicago Press, 1975), 22.

55. *Lectures on the Foundations of Mathematics*, 14.

56. LW to Sraffa, 21 February 1934, in Moira De Iaco, "Wittgenstein to Sraffa: Two Newly-Discovered Letters from February and March 1934," *Nordic Wittgenstein Review* 8, nos. 1–2 (2019): 217.

57. LW to Sraffa, 11 March 1934, in De Iaco "Wittgenstein to Sraffa," 220.

58. Hermine to LW, 18 October 1947, in WFL, 263.

59. Gretl to LW, late 1942, in WFL, 247.

60. Hermine to Hänsel, 1938, in *Ludwig Hänsel—Ludwig Wittgenstein: Eine Freundschaft*, ed. Ilse Somavilla, Anton Unterkircher, and Christian Paul Berger (Innsbruck: Haymon, 1994), 151.

61. "Wittgenstein's 1938 Preface," in *Wittgenstein After His Nachlass*, ed. Nuno Venturinha (Basingstoke: Palgrave Macmillan, 2010), 187.

62. LW, 1938, in MS 160, 4.

63. WIC, 293n; LW to Raymond Townsend, 15 October 1939, in WIC, 311.

64. LW, 13 June 1940, in MS 117; Ray Monk, DG, 428.

65. LW, 28 December 1941, in MS 125; LW, 11 July 1948, in MS 137.

66. Ronald MacKeith, "Ludwig Wittgenstein," in POW, 716.

67. Leo Kinlen, "Wittgenstein in Newcastle," in POW, 723; Fouracre to LW, 15 January 1945, in GBW; LW to Fouracre, 21 October 1946, in GBW.

68. LW to Malcolm, 11 September 1943, in WIC, 357; LW to Rhees, 17 October 1944, in WIC, 367.

69. Knut Tranøy, "Wittgenstein in Cambridge, 1949–51: Some Personal Recollections," in POW, 1021; LW to Moore, 3 December 1946, in WIC, 405.

70. LW to Moore, 7 March 1941, in WIC, 341.

71. "Arthur MacIver's Diary: Cambridge (October 1929–March 1930)," ed. Brian McGuinness, *Wittgenstein-Studien* 7 (2016): 251.

72. Norman Malcolm, LWAM, 57.

73. Karl Popper, *Unended Quest* (London: Routledge, 1992), 142.

74. Minutes of the Moral Sciences Club, 26 October 1946, in WIC, 402.

75. Popper, *Unended Quest*, 141–42.

76. LW to Rhees, 28 October 1946, in WIC, 403.

77. LW, 19 November 1946, in MS 133; LW to Richards, 1 November 1946, in ONB; LW, 22 July 1946, in MS 130; LW, 8 August 1946, in MS 130.

78. LW, 8 October 1946, in MS 132; LW, 27 November 1946, in MS 133.

79. LW to Richards, 11 April 1951, in ONB.

80. LW to Helene, 24 November 1946, in WFL, 259.

81. Tranøy, "Wittgenstein in Cambridge," in POW, 1022; LW, 13–14 April 1947, in C&V, 69, 70.

82. G. H. von Wright, *Wittgenstein* (Oxford: Blackwell, 1982), 11.

83. LW to von Wright, 23 February 1948, in WIC, 423; LW to Malcolm, 5 February 1948, in WIC, 422; LW to Richards, 5 March 1948, in ONB.

84. LW to Malcolm, 15 March 1948, in WIC, 424; LW to Richards, 1 and 14 December 1948, in ONB (film title corrected); LW, 2 April 1947, in C&V, 65–66; LW to Malcolm, 14 June 1949, in WIC, 446.

85. Drury, "Conversations with Wittgenstein," in POW, 828.

86. LW, 25 February 1949, in MS 138.

87. LW to Rhees, 31 August 1949, in GBW.

88. William H. Gass, "A Memory of a Master," in POW, 967; Harry Frankfurt, "Reflections of My Career in Philosophy," *Proceedings and Addresses of the American Philosophical Association* 85, no. 2 (November 2011): 94.

89. LW to Richards, 10 October 1949, in ONB (erroneously dated by LW as September).

90. LW to Rhees, 3 January 1950, in WIC, 455.

91. LW to Richards, 7 February 1950, in ONB.

92. Stephen Leach, "Chadbourne Gilpatric and Ludwig Wittgenstein: A Fateful Meeting," *Nordic Wittgenstein Review* 9 (2020): 214.

93. O. K. Bouwsma, *Wittgenstein: Conversations, 1949–51*, ed. J. L. Craft and Ronald E. Hustwit (Indianapolis: Hackett, 1986), 73; G. E. M. Anscombe, *From Plato to Wittgenstein: Essays by G. E. M. Anscombe*, ed. Mary Geach and Luke Gormally (Exeter: Imprint Academic, 2011), 169.

94. Rush Rhees, *Wittgenstein and the Possibility of Discourse* (Oxford: Blackwell, 2006), 262.

95. LW, *Philosophy of Psychology—A Fragment*, xi, §315 (PI, 233).

96. James C. Klagge, "Wittgenstein, Science, and the Evolution of Concepts," in *Wittgenstein and Scientism*, ed. Jonathan Beale and Ian James Kidd (London: Routledge, 2017), 193–208.

97. LW to Richards, 17 March 1951, in ONB.

98. LW, *On Certainty*, ed. G. E. M. Anscombe and G. H. von Wright (Oxford: Blackwell, 1969), §675–76.

99. LW to Richards, 4 April 1951, in ONB.

100. LW to Rhees, 14 March 1951, in WIC, 475 (spelling corrected); Mary Scrutton (later known as Mary Midgley), "How Charming Is Divine Philosophy?" *New Statesman and Nation*, 10 March 1951, 278.

101. Joan Bevan, "Wittgenstein's Last Year," in POW, 1030, 1031.

102. Richards to LW, 23 April 1951, in ONB; LW to Richards, 11 April 1951, in ONB.

103. Von Wright, "Biographical Sketch," in Norman Malcolm, LWAM, 18; Pascal, "A Personal Memoir," in POW, 535; Norman Malcolm, LWAM, 81.

104. Norman Malcolm, LWAM, 84n4; LW, 24 October 1931, in MS 183.

105. LW, 19 December 1929, in MS 108.

106. Lettice Ramsey to Friedrich Hayek, 1953, in Nicole Immler, *Das Familiengedächtnis Der Wittgensteins* (Bielefeld: Transkript Verlag, 2011), 160; LW to Malcolm, 16 November 1944, in WIC, 370; Frances Partridge, *Love in Bloomsbury: Memoirs* (Boston: Little, Brown, 1981), 160; Malcolm, "Ludwig Wittgenstein: A Symposium," in POW, 1050; Paul Engelmann, LFLW, 66; C. D. Broad, "Review of Norman Malcolm, *Ludwig Wittgenstein: A Memoir*," *Universities Quarterly* 13, no. 3 (May 1959): 306.

107. LW, WIC, 241n; Ambrose to Mrs. G. E. Moore, 8 February 1936, in Immler, *Familiengedächtnis Der Wittgensteins*, 162.

108. Drury, "Ludwig Wittgenstein: A Symposium," in POW, 1044; Dr. Edward Bevan to Sister Mary Elwyn McHale, 30 August 1966, held at Cornell University Library, Division of Rare and

Manuscript Collections; Franz Parak, quoted in Brian McGuinness, YL, 269; C. L. Stevenson to LW, 18 November 1933, in WIC, 214.

Chapter 7. A Head Full of Question Marks

1. Ryle, "Ludwig Wittgenstein," *Analysis* 12, no. 1 (October 1951): 8–9.

2. Russell, "Ludwig Wittgenstein," *Mind* 60, no. 239 (July 1951): 298; Bertrand Russell, *Portraits from Memory* (London: Allen & Unwin, 1956), 156.

3. P. F. Strawson, "Critical Notice: *Philosophical Investigations* by Ludwig Wittgenstein," *Mind* 63, no. 249 (January 1954): 99; Russell, "Philosophical Analysis," in *My Philosophical Development* (London: Allen & Unwin, 1959), 216–17; Rupert Crawshay-Williams, *Russell Remembered* (Oxford: Oxford University Press, 1970), 78; Russell, *Portraits from Memory*, 26.

4. Anthony Kenny, *The Legacy of Wittgenstein* (Oxford: Blackwell, 1984), vii. See also P. M. S. Hacker, *Wittgenstein's Place in Twentieth-Century Analytic Philosophy* (Oxford: Blackwell, 1996), ch. 8.

5. LW, TLP 4.112.

6. Russell, *An Outline of Philosophy* (1927) (London: Unwin, 1970), 1.

7. O. K. Bouwsma, *Wittgenstein: Conversations, 1949–51*, ed. J. L. Craft and Ronald E. Hustwit (Indianapolis: Hackett, 1986), 48; Russell, *Portraits from Memory*, 26.

8. Waismann to Schlick, 9 August 1934, in *The Voices of Wittgenstein: The Vienna Circle*, ed. Gordon Baker (London: Routledge, 2003), xxvii.

9. Drury, "Conversations with Wittgenstein," in POW, 836.

FURTHER READING

For more detailed treatments of Wittgenstein's philosophy, I recommend the following books.

Good short books for beginners are P. M. S. Hacker, *Wittgenstein* (London: Weidenfeld & Nicolson, 2021); Ray Monk, *How to Read Wittgenstein* (New York: Norton, 2005); and James Klagge, *Simply Wittgenstein* (New York: Simply Charly, 2016).

For fuller introductory treatments, see William Child, *Wittgenstein* (London: Routledge, 2011); and P. M. S. Hacker, *Wittgenstein's Place in Twentieth-Century Analytic Philosophy* (Oxford: Blackwell, 1996).

A more advanced study is *A Companion to Wittgenstein*, ed. Hans-Johann Glock and John Hyman (Oxford: Wiley Blackwell, 2017).

ACKNOWLEDGMENTS

THE RESEARCH for this book unwittingly began in the 1970s in Cambridge, where some of my teachers were former pupils of Wittgenstein. I cannot now name everyone who has since then helped me to think about him. For recent assistance and support, I thank the warden and fellows of All Souls College, Oxford, who provided an ideal environment for study, and Angelika von Hase, who helped with German sources. I am most grateful to Edmund Fawcett, Nick Griffin, Paul Horwich, James Klagge, Richard Robb, David Stern, and Chaim Tannenbaum for their comments on the manuscript, to Radmila Schweitzer of the Wittgenstein Initiative in Vienna for unfailing assistance, and to the following for helpful correspondence or discussion: Kenneth Blackwell, Peter Eigner, Anthony Grayling, Peter Hacker, Cecilia Heyes, Nicole Immler, Allan Janik, Sara Lipton, Cheryl Misak, Ray Monk, Georg Predota, the late Peter Pulzer, Alfred Schmidt, Joachim Schulte, Elana Shapira, Barry Smith, Jan Swafford, and Sarah Watling. I am also grateful to Ileene Smith for commissioning the book, and for her patience, and to the staff of Yale University Press.

INDEX

Note: Page numbers in italics indicate photographs.

Jewish Lives is a prizewinning series of interpretative biography designed to explore the many facets of Jewish identity. Individual volumes illuminate the imprint of Jewish figures upon literature, religion, philosophy, politics, cultural and economic life, and the arts and sciences. Subjects are paired with authors to elicit lively, deeply informed books that explore the range and depth of the Jewish experience from antiquity to the present.

Jewish Lives is a partnership of Yale University Press and the Leon D. Black Foundation. Ileene Smith is editorial director. Anita Shapira and Steven J. Zipperstein are series editors.

PUBLISHED TITLES INCLUDE:

Abraham: The First Jew, by Anthony Julius
Rabbi Akiva: Sage of the Talmud, by Barry W. Holtz
Ben-Gurion: Father of Modern Israel, by Anita Shapira
Judah Benjamin: Counselor to the Confederacy, by James Traub
Bernard Berenson: A Life in the Picture Trade, by Rachel Cohen
Irving Berlin: New York Genius, by James Kaplan
Sarah: The Life of Sarah Bernhardt, by Robert Gottlieb
Leonard Bernstein: An American Musician, by Allen Shawn
Hayim Nahman Bialik: Poet of Hebrew, by Avner Holtzman
Léon Blum: Prime Minister, Socialist, Zionist, by Pierre Birnbaum
Franz Boas: In Praise of Open Minds, by Noga Arikha
Louis D. Brandeis: American Prophet, by Jeffrey Rosen
Mel Brooks: Disobedient Jew, by Jeremy Dauber
Martin Buber: A Life of Faith and Dissent, by Paul Mendes-Flohr
David: The Divided Heart, by David Wolpe
Moshe Dayan: Israel's Controversial Hero, by Mordechai Bar-On
Disraeli: The Novel Politician, by David Cesarani
Alfred Dreyfus: The Man at the Center of the Affair, by Maurice Samuels
Einstein: His Space and Times, by Steven Gimbel
Becoming Elijah: Prophet of Transformation, by Daniel Matt
The Many Lives of Anne Frank, by Ruth Franklin
Becoming Freud: The Making of a Psychoanalyst, by Adam Phillips
Betty Friedan: Magnificent Disrupter, by Rachel Shteir

Emma Goldman: Revolution as a Way of Life, by Vivian Gornick
Hank Greenberg: The Hero Who Didn't Want to Be One, by Mark Kurlansky
Peggy Guggenheim: The Shock of the Modern, by Francine Prose
Ben Hecht: Fighting Words, Moving Pictures, by Adina Hoffman
Heinrich Heine: Writing the Revolution, by George Prochnik
Lillian Hellman: An Imperious Life, by Dorothy Gallagher
Herod the Great: Jewish King in a Roman World, by Martin Goodman
Theodor Herzl: The Charismatic Leader, by Derek Penslar
Abraham Joshua Heschel: A Life of Radical Amazement, by Julian Zelizer
Houdini: The Elusive American, by Adam Begley
Jabotinsky: A Life, by Hillel Halkin
Jacob: Unexpected Patriarch, by Yair Zakovitch
Franz Kafka: The Poet of Shame and Guilt, by Saul Friedländer
Carole King: She Made the Earth Move, by Jane Eisner
Rav Kook: Mystic in a Time of Revolution, by Yehudah Mirsky
Stanley Kubrick: American Filmmaker, by David Mikics
Stan Lee: A Life in Comics, by Liel Leibovitz
Primo Levi: The Matter of a Life, by Berel Lang
Maimonides: Faith in Reason, by Alberto Manguel
Groucho Marx: The Comedy of Existence, by Lee Siegel
Karl Marx: Philosophy and Revolution, by Shlomo Avineri
Louis B. Mayer and Irving Thalberg: The Whole Equation, by Kenneth Turan
Golda Meir: Israel's Matriarch, by Deborah E. Lipstadt
Menasseh ben Israel: Rabbi of Amsterdam, by Steven Nadler
Moses Mendelssohn: Sage of Modernity, by Shmuel Feiner
Harvey Milk: His Lives and Death, by Lillian Faderman
Arthur Miller: American Witness, by John Lahr

Moses: A Human Life, by Avivah Gottlieb Zornberg
Amos Oz: Writer, Activist, Icon, by Robert Alter
Proust: The Search, by Benjamin Taylor
Yitzhak Rabin: Soldier, Leader, Statesman, by Itamar Rabinovich
Ayn Rand: Writing a Gospel of Success, by Alexandra Popoff
Walther Rathenau: Weimar's Fallen Statesman, by Shulamit Volkov
Man Ray: The Artist and His Shadows, by Arthur Lubow
Sidney Reilly: Master Spy, by Benny Morris
Admiral Hyman Rickover: Engineer of Power, by Marc Wortman
Jerome Robbins: A Life in Dance, by Wendy Lesser
Julius Rosenwald: Repairing the World, by Hasia R. Diner
Philip Roth: Stung by Life, by Steven J. Zipperstein
Mark Rothko: Toward the Light in the Chapel, by Annie Cohen-Solal
Ruth: A Migrant's Tale, by Ilana Pardes
Menachem Mendel Schneerson: Becoming the Messiah, by Ezra Glinter
Gershom Scholem: Master of the Kabbalah, by David Biale
Bugsy Siegel: The Dark Side of the American Dream, by Michael Shnayerson
Solomon: The Lure of Wisdom, by Steven Weitzman
Steven Spielberg: A Life in Films, by Molly Haskell
Spinoza: Freedom's Messiah, by Ian Buruma
Alfred Stieglitz: Taking Pictures, Making Painters, by Phyllis Rose
Barbra Streisand: Redefining Beauty, Femininity, and Power, by Neal Gabler
Henrietta Szold: Hadassah and the Zionist Dream, by Francine Klagsbrun
Leon Trotsky: A Revolutionary's Life, by Joshua Rubenstein
Warner Bros: The Making of an American Movie Studio, by David Thomson

Elie Wiesel: Confronting the Silence, by Joseph Berger
Ludwig Wittgenstein: Philosophy in the Age of Airplanes, by Anthony Gottlieb

FORTHCOMING TITLES INCLUDE:

Hannah Arendt, by Masha Gessen
The Ba'al Shem Tov, by Ariel Mayse
Walter Benjamin, by Peter E. Gordon
Bob Dylan, by Sasha Frere-Jones
George Gershwin, by Gary Giddins
Ruth Bader Ginsburg, by Jeffrey Rosen
Jesus, by Jack Miles
Josephus, by Daniel Boyarin
Louis Kahn, by Gini Alhadeff
Mordecai Kaplan, by Jenna Weissman Joselit
Henry Kissinger, by Dennis Ross
Fiorello La Guardia, by Brenda Wineapple
Mahler, by Leon Botstein
Norman Mailer, by David Bromwich
Robert Oppenheimer, by David Rieff
Rebecca, by Judith Shulevitz
Edmond de Rothschild, by James McAuley
Jonas Salk, by David Margolick
Stephen Sondheim, by Daniel Okrent
Susan Sontag, by Benjamin Taylor
Gertrude Stein, by Lauren Elkin
Sabbatai Tsevi, by Pawel Maciejko
Billy Wilder, by Noah Isenberg